California
Houses

"Architecture, too, has an ulterior motive always lurking around the corner, the idea of creating paradise. That is the only purpose of our buildings. If we did not carry this idea with us all through our lives, our buildings would all be simpler and more trivial, and life would be—well, would there be life at all? Every building, every architectural product that is its symbol, is intended to show that we wish to build a paradise on earth for man."

—Alvar Aalto

California Houses

Creativity in Context

Michael Webb

With 345 illustrations

Contents

Introduction

I have selected 36 houses that capture the spirit of California in distinctive ways and respond creatively to context and the environment. Nearly all were shaped by a dialogue between owner and architect, as well as the site and budget. Large or small, urban or rural, they demonstrate the extraordinary range of invention emerging from the offices of established and younger architects. This is a celebration of the best talent as well as clients with the courage, imagination, and means to commission houses that are one-of-a-kind and advance the art of architecture. Architects need public attention to build their practice; enlightened patrons deserve it—for their vision and for setting an example that may inspire their peers.

The houses are grouped into three thematic sections: Engaging Nature, Weaving the Urban Fabric, and Viewing Town & Country. These categories are porous, and some residences could be placed in more than one. Though each of these houses has a unique personality, there are common features that recur. In California a high level of sustainability is mandated by progressive legislation and reinforced by the desire of architects and responsible owners to do the right thing. All of these houses employ active and passive strategies to reduce their carbon footprint. There is a strong emphasis on natural light and ventilation, thermal insulation, solar and photovoltaic panels, and rainwater collection for irrigation. They are constructed to conserve energy, withstand earthquakes, and, often, to resist wildfires. Glass sliders blur the boundaries between indoor and outdoor living, especially in the southern half of the state. There is a focus on materiality and frequent references to the local vernacular, alongside daring explorations of complex geometries.

Why limit the choice to just one of the fifty States of the Union? In part because California is a magnet for wealth and talent, and excels in residential architecture, even as it trails behind New England and even parts of the Midwest in new civic, institutional, and commercial buildings. The boom years may be over, along with the buoyant optimism of the post-war decades, but the name still casts a spell. Joni Mitchell sang poignantly of coming home to California, and that ballad expresses the timeless appeal of a state that has had a mythical dimension ever since the name was coined in a Spanish romance five centuries ago. The author described an island of Black women warriors, ruled by a queen and decked out in gold, located to the east of the Indies. Soon after its publication, Spanish explorers sailing up the west coast of Mexico supposed the peninsula of Baja California to be that island.

In 1579, Sir Francis Drake put ashore near San Francisco Bay, naming the land Nova Albion and claiming it for Queen Elizabeth I. Colonized two centuries later by settlers from Spain and Mexico, the territory was ceded to the United States in 1848—the year a new wave of immigrants was lured by the discovery of gold. Incorporated as the 31st State of the Union in 1850, California's population grew exponentially. Native tribes were decimated, and the total of new residents increased from around 8,000 to nearly 40 million today.

Speculators and boosters portrayed California as an earthly paradise, and the fantasies spun by Hollywood entranced the world. It was a place to start over and make a new life—for émigrés from the Midwest, Europe, Asia, and Latin America. During the Great Depression of the 1930s the movies provided employment and entertainment, and the state was a refuge for farmers from the Dust Bowl as well as European writers and artists fleeing Hitler. Millions of servicemen shipped out to war in the Pacific from ports in California and returned to settle there and start families. The population has increased four-fold since 1950, and only now shows signs of having peaked. Silicon Valley has delivered fortunes immeasurably greater than any prospector could have imagined. This is a state that is constantly threatened by earthquakes, wildfires, and record droughts alternating with violent storms. And yet the myths endure. Gold and oil, early sources of prosperity, were celebrated in black and yellow auto plates, a design that was retired and then revived to be used as a customized status symbol on black Escalades, Teslas, and the ubiquitous BMWs. Celebrities and billionaires abound, and an industry has grown up to chronicle their extravagance and their trophy houses in Beverly Hills and Malibu. What matter if the glamor is paper-thin and unrepresentative of the population at large. To quote from John Ford's elegiac movie *The Man Who Shot Liberty Valance* (1962), "This is the West. When legend becomes fact, print the legend."

The same contradictions are evident in residential architecture. There can be no singular ideal in a state that is larger and more varied than Japan and nearly all European countries. It is about 900 miles (1,450 km) in length, the distance from London to Barcelona. Within its 163,696 square miles (423,970 km²) are some of the world's hottest deserts, oldest redwood groves, a spectacular coastline, snowcapped mountains, a fertile central valley, and the urban sprawl of Los Angeles and San Francisco. Early settlers imported the building styles of their homelands, from haciendas to Queen Anne and Cape Cod; the hybrid dubbed "Mediterranean" is still a popular choice. The state remains in thrall to traditional forms, inventing a history where none existed. Homeowners' associations resist change and impose conformity to preserve this fresh-minted legacy.

For most Californians the choice of shelter is determined by whatever is close to hand and affordable, from a rental apartment to a tract house. Meanwhile, too many people are being priced out of major cities, and a growing number are homeless or struggling to keep a roof over their heads. At the opposite end of the economic spectrum there is a growing demand for houses that have a character as strong as their owner

and location. A lucky few can choose to live where they want and commission an architect to tailor one or more houses to their dreams, remodeling an existing property or building ground-up. Though still a tiny niche in the market—one in ten thousand, perhaps—this is a model of how most people might prefer to live if they had the means and independence of mind.

Many of these houses are located in or around Los Angeles, which has a been a cradle of innovation in residential architecture for more than a century, exerting its influence worldwide. At the beginning of the twentieth century, the California bungalow was a cheap and practical variant on the costly Arts and Crafts houses of Charles and Henry Greene. In the 1910s, Irving Gill was inspired by the white walls and rounded arches of Spanish Mission churches to build proto-modern houses with flat roofs and thin concrete walls. Frank Lloyd Wright declared he was creating a new California architecture, drawing on pre-Columbian forms and ornament, and employing concrete in novel ways. The Hollyhock House (1920) is a masterpiece; the textile block houses that followed are picturesque but fragile.

R. M. Schindler left Vienna in 1914 to work in Chicago and then for Wright in LA, before embarking on an inventive 30-year practice that began with a house—studio of tilt-up concrete panels and redwood in what is now West Hollywood. Inspired by a camping trip, it was an experiment in collective living for the Schindlers and another couple. A century later, it is still a radical concept.

Richard Neutra served his apprenticeship with Erich Mendelsohn in Berlin, spent a year with Wright and briefly shared Schindler's base in the mid-1920s. They split acrimoniously, and Neutra made his mark with the Lovell Health House (1929), a landmark of the International Style. Schindler continued to reinvent himself with every new commission; Neutra played variations on a theme that remained remarkably consistent for the next 40 years, while nurturing the careers of Gregory Ain and Harwell Hamilton Harris, among many other talented Modernists.

In 1945, the Case Study House program was launched by John Entenza, editor of the influential *Arts & Architecture* magazine, in the hope that the 36 designs (25 of which were realized) would be replicated on a large scale. The impact of these prototypes, notably the steel-framed houses of Craig Ellwood and Pierre Koenig, and the prefabricated assemblage of Charles & Ray Eames, was wide and enduring. Entenza was a cautious patron who favored orthogonal post-and-beam architecture —a warmer, softer version of the International Style— hoping it would win broad acceptance. In that regard he was disappointed; crowds attended his open houses, but the prices were too high for most potential buyers. It was left to the enlightened developer Joseph Eichler to create estates of standardized Modernist homes, mostly in northern California.

Arts & Architecture was progressive up to a point, but it ignored such brilliant mavericks as Schindler and John Lautner, as did the East Coast journals and the architectural establishment. History repeated itself a decade later, when Frank Gehry was mocked for his use of exposed beams, plywood, chain link, and daring geometries. Only his artist friends and a few perceptive critics recognized his genius until the Bilbao Guggenheim (1997) and Walt Disney Concert Hall (2003) silenced the doubters. By then his practice was well established and he had little time to design houses. His current residence, featured here (see p. 37), was designed by his son, Sam.

Today, LA may have as high a concentration of gifted architects as New York, but a greater proportion of them are focused on single-family and multi-unit housing. Though empty and affordable sites are scarce (most are tear-downs) and nimbyism is a recurring obstacle, LA still offers some of the same opportunities to try something new as it did a century ago. The city authorities, university presidents, and developers nearly always settle for the conventional and second-rate, and the planning department is sclerotic, but it takes only a few bold individuals and institutions to draw on the pool of design talent and create a new landmark.

The challenge is greater in San Francisco, which is as conservative in aesthetics as it is progressive in morality and politics. For a century following the Gold Rush it was the most prestigious urban hub west of the Mississippi. It was rebuilt as a Beaux-Arts City Beautiful following the earthquake and fire of 1906, giving its downtown and prosperous districts a handsome urbanity. It also had a strong working-class component and a rambunctious waterfront, but it has gentrified to a greater degree than Manhattan and become narcissistic. That chokes off the invention one would expect from an affluent metropolis fertilized by the architecture department of University of California (UC), Berkeley, and enriched by the proximity of Silicon Valley.

The first wave of Modernism passed San Francisco by: Neutra, Schindler, and their protégés built almost nothing in the Bay Area and no local architect offered a progressive alternative. Nostalgia for Arts and Crafts and Spanish Colonial was dominant until after World War II. William Wurster, Joseph Esherick, and William Turnbull Jr. created a woodsy version of Modernism, rooted in the traditional architecture of the Bay Area— what Professor Kenneth Frampton would call "critical regionalism." There was no Frank Gehry or Thom Mayne to lead, nor a school as radical as the Southern California Institute of Architecture to challenge conventions.

In the past few decades, a new generation of architects has opened offices in San Francisco and broken with the woodsy tradition. They are creating sophisticated houses south to Carmel, north to Mendocino, and even, stealthily, in the city. Constrained by protective local ordinances, they have enriched urban streets and rustic enclaves, and their creativity is evident throughout this anthology.

Beyond these two big cities are mountains and deserts, forests and rural communities that offer a retreat from urban pressures for those who seek the embrace of nature as a way of life or as a weekend retreat. A prime example is Sea Ranch (1960s), a planned community on the rugged shore of Sonoma County. Its original buildings by Joseph Esherick and the firm Moore, Lyndon, Turnbull, and Whittaker, with landscaping by Lawrence Halprin, are a model of environmental, site-specific design. To the south, in Big Sur, Micky Muennig integrated his organic houses within a setting of matchless beauty, often embedding them in the land or raising them into treetops. Visitors to the luxury resort of Post Ranch can share the experience of his houses on a larger scale.

Most Californian architects take pride in making their buildings sustainable, but that has now become the only way to secure a permit. In recent decades, state and local authorities have set an example to the rest of America, introducing mandates to protect trees, wildlife, and the coastline, to conserve energy and water, and to make every new building environmentally responsible, even net-zero. California is already suffering the effects of climate change, with worse to come, but it is making a determined effort to fight back.

ENGAGING NATURE

The more we crowd into large cities the more we crave some element of nature, even if it is no more than a few potted plants or a pocket garden. That enhances the appeal of a retreat into the countryside; a place where nature rules. Thanks to the internet, a rustic retreat can now become a place in which to live and work year-round, encouraging architects to design second houses that are as versatile and commodious as the most ambitious urban dwellings, as well as snug cabins for a weekend escape.

The challenge is to protect the qualities that people have come far to enjoy. Unregulated development can quickly transform wilderness into suburban sprawl, as happened in and around Palm Springs. The house that Neutra built there for the Kaufmanns in 1947 was a winter retreat at the edge of a tiny community, but air conditioning brought a rash of tract homes and a host of permanent residents. Yet, even in built-up areas, architects can orient houses toward a patch of greenery and landscape designers can create the illusion of a rural setting.

Selected for their diversity, these houses respond to every kind of landscape, from tumbling rocks to pounding surf and the dappled light of forests. One straddles a creek, another is elevated to protect tree roots, a third steps down a wooded slope. They pay homage to traditional forms and the pure lines of minimalist sculpture. Roofless House (see p. 75) shuts out neighboring properties to focus attention on treetops and the sky, while Hill House (see p. 17) creates its own landscape: a mound planted with succulents, hollowed out to contain soaring volumes and inner patios.

Hill House Montecito

SHUBINDONALDSON ARCHITECTS

Photographs might suggest that a spaceship has landed and sprouted greenery to disguise its presence in this leafy community south of Santa Barbara. In fact, the house was conceived as a grand marriage of architecture and nature, a concrete shell on arched supports embedded in the landscape and planted with succulents. Its enclosed spaces, terraces, and patios cover 19,000 square feet (1,765 m²), but it passes unnoticed from the street and reveals its scale and structure only as you get close. Designed to withstand wildfires, floods, and earthquakes, it draws its power from a solar array to achieve net-zero energy use.

Bruce Heavin commissioned Robin Donaldson to design recording studios for his film company, enjoyed the experience, and selected him to create this house. As a graduate of Art Center College of Design who shares a passion for art with his wife, Lynda Weinman, Heavin wanted something unconventional. Donaldson drafted a design for a different site before his clients switched to this gently inclined four-acre lot. They drove around on a cherry picker to explore its potential and realized that a rooftop only 16-feet (4.9 m) high would command sweeping views of ocean and mountains. "Why don't we bury the whole thing?" said Heavin, and that opened up a whole range of possibilities. He gave his architect a free hand but remained fully involved in the creative process. Donaldson sketched different iterations, simplifying complex forms, until Heavin said, "I think this needs to get built."

There are echoes of John Lautner's Elrod House (1968) in the shallow concrete dome and circular plan, as well as the muscularity of the structure. But the concept is radically different, as the owners wanted the house to feel as though it had been carved out of a solid block.

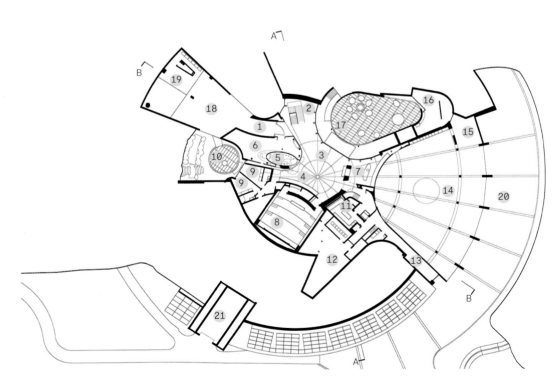

LOWER-FLOOR PLAN

1 Art entry
2 Gallery
3 Game room
4 Library
5 Light well
6 Reading room
7 Lower-floor bar
8 Media room
9 Guest room
10 Guest patio
11 Laundry room
12 Mechanical room
13 Service
14 Garage
15 Garage workshop
16 Painting studio
17 Avocado courtyard
18 Pottery courtyard
19 Pottery shop
20 Lower motorcourt
21 Pool equipment

CALIFORNIA HOUSES

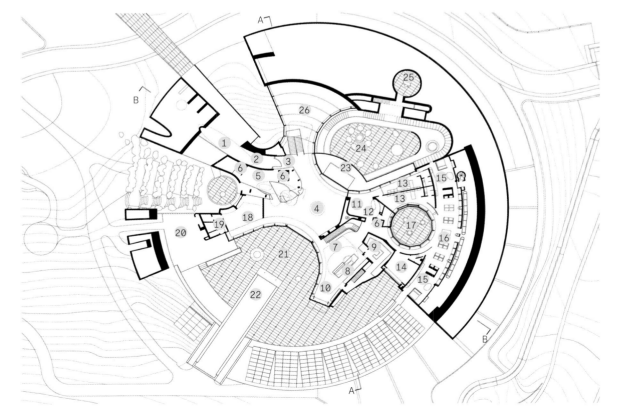

UPPER-FLOOR PLAN

1 Entry bridge
2 Threshold
3 Main entry
4 Great room
5 Light well
6 Powder room
7 Daily living area
8 Daily kitchen
9 Prep kitchen
10 Dining room
11 Family room
12 Upper-floor bar
13 Office
14 Primary bedroom
15 Primary bathroom
16 Primary closet
17 Primary courtyard
18 Gym
19 Changing room
20 Pool cabaña
21 Pool deck
22 Pool
23 Avocado bridge
24 Avocado courtyard
25 Sculpture hole
26 Gallery

ENGAGING NATURE

It emerges from the ground and rises to enclose soaring spaces and sunken courtyards. One of these voids is studded with sandstone boulders excavated on site—rocks that were formed when the ocean retreated millions of years ago—and configured as seating for an amphitheater. A gridded metal bridge with a cutaway canopy leads to the main entrance: a massive ovoid door of glass, framed in steel, with exposed hinges that are intricate works of industrial art (right).

The expansive great room is a symphony of curves on plan and in the openings that lead on to other parts of the house. It is a versatile arena for entertaining that is bathed in natural light from an oculus and from tilt-up, room-height windows. One of these opens onto a terrace and ocean breezes flow through, keeping the house cool on all but a few days of summer. Around the entry, folds in the glass capture a kaleidoscope of reflections. Curvilinear walls of plastered steel studs are scooped out in places, and one of these contains a James Turrell light work that is constantly changing color. Other artworks are strategically deployed, and Janet Echelman created a site-specific skein of fabric that is draped across one side of the room. The white shell domesticates the concrete frame, but some of the steel structure (still with the builders' marks) is left exposed, and suspended pipes can support speakers or lights when the room is a stage for events. As Heavin notes, "the furniture is easily moved out and we've hosted dinner for as many as 170 people."

Donaldson used the circle as an ordering device from the start, but Weinman confesses that she was initially terrified by the prospect of living in a bubble. "Bruce had never been so happy, so I made my peace with it and asked only that they build a studio where I could make ceramics on a more ambitious scale," she recalls. "Now it's complete I'm overjoyed—the house never seems too big and I feel comfortable even when I'm alone." And the house proved equally rewarding for the architect, who is exploring the ideas it inspired in other commissions. Were Kubla Khan to come back to life and search for another stately pleasure dome he would be overjoyed.

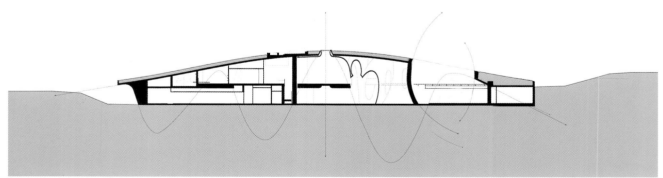

SECTION B

CALIFORNIA HOUSES

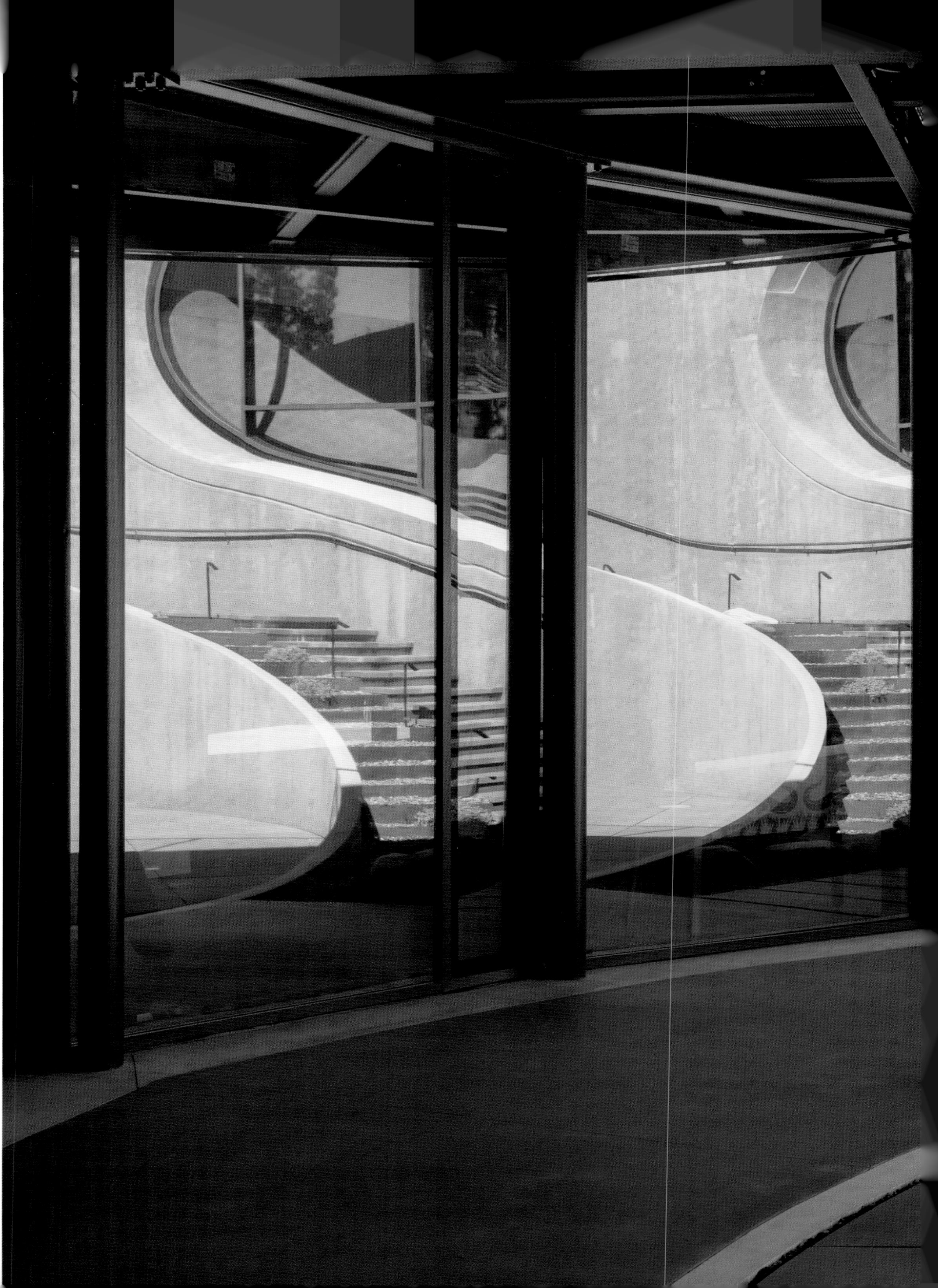

Suspension House
Northern California

FOUGERON ARCHITECTURE

A sophisticated, art-loving couple who cherish seclusion and have
a young daughter found an ideal retreat: an old wood house
that straddled a creek at the foot of a rocky canyon. It backed up
to a waterfall and trees shut out views of neighboring houses.
Although it is no longer legal in California to build this way, you are
permitted to remodel existing structures, so the couple commissioned
Anne Fougeron to turn it into a minimalist residence of steel and glass.
A third floor was added, increasing the floor area to 2,500 square feet
(232.3 m²), while remaining within the same footprint and incorporating
parts of the old. The architect had demonstrated her skill in the
Fall House, which cascades down a precipitous slope above the ocean
in Big Sur, but that was all-new and solidly grounded, while this was
a hybrid that proved even more demanding.

The old house had rotted away and was supported on columns.
After heavy rains the creek becomes a raging torrent, carrying rocks
and logs that could dislodge these supports. To upgrade the structure
it was necessary to remove the columns and suspend it above the
water. Fougeron brought in Paul Endres, a brilliant structural engineer
and a former student of hers at UC Berkeley. "He understands
our architectural vocabulary and how to make it work," she explains.
"He treated it as a suspension bridge with three steel modules drilled
up to 20 feet [6 m] into the bedrock on either side of the canyon
supporting a steel frame beneath the original floors. A lot of the
engineering is exposed, and we considered it important to show how
the structure works."

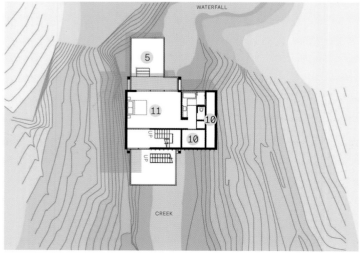

FIRST-FLOOR PLAN

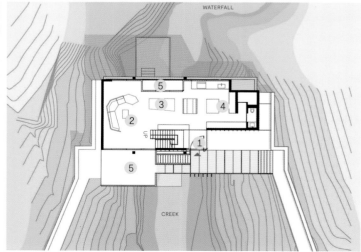

SECOND-FLOOR PLAN

CALIFORNIA HOUSES

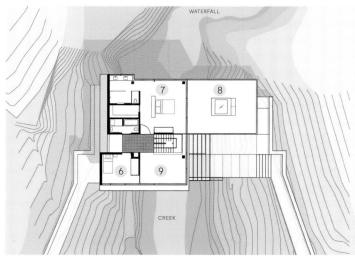

THIRD-FLOOR PLAN

1	Entry
2	Living area
3	Dining area
4	Kitchen
5	Deck
6	Bedroom
7	Primary suite
8	Roof deck
9	Flex space
10	Utilities
11	Guest suite

ENGAGING NATURE

CALIFORNIA HOUSES

Suspending the house in mid-air brought fresh challenges. All the connections, from services to the septic tank, had to be refabricated. The materials were carefully weighed to ensure they would not overload the supports. And the house had to be fire-resistant because there is no room for trucks to turn on the narrow road that leads to the carport and the steps going down to the house. Rooftop solar panels and storage batteries provide most of the power; high-performance glass and extra insulation reduce consumption. Mechanical services are housed in the lower floor and in a detached steel guest house that doubles as a studio.

The owners were intimately involved in the creative process, scrutinizing every aspect of the design and making clear their preference for expansive glazing and steel, as well as an austere monochromatic palette, though stone is used on the boundary walls. The house is entered at the mid-level through the living areas. Interior and exterior stairs lead down to a guest bedroom that doubles as an office, and up to the primary suite and child's bedroom. Each floor opens onto decks through glass sliders that incorporate mesh screens to keep mosquitos at bay. On the first two floors, structure and orientation follow that of the old house, but the new third floor is rotated 90 degrees to lighten the composition and better relate to the site. A cantilevered roof shades the glass, and exterior roll-down blinds block the westerly sun. Light and airy, the house has a sense of buoyancy and—as on a suspension bridge—there is a slight sway on windy days.

Richard Neutra described his residential work as "a machine in the garden," juxtaposing orthogonal architecture and organic plantings. Suspension House carries that concept to its limit. In contrast to Frank Lloyd Wright's Fallingwater (1935), where the waterfall is an off-stage presence, this house is transparent and only 22-feet (6.7 m) deep so the cascade is front and center, and the glass frames a wall of greenery. At times it can feel like a tropical rain forest. That softens the sharp angles and austere surfaces, complementing the rigor of the industrial aesthetic. As Fougeron observes, "Every site is different and elicits a different response. Here you are reminded how precious some sites can be and are inspired to enrich them with the best possible architecture."

CALIFORNIA HOUSES

Adelaide House Santa Monica

GEHRY PARTNERS

A recent arrival on a sedate street overlooking Santa Monica Canyon respects the scale of its neighbors, but is set apart on a rise behind olive trees and a bed of lavender. Two fully glazed, angled wings extend forward and converge on the entry. Above is a jumble of gables, copper-clad in reference to the red-tiled roofs that abound on this street. A stone entry arch, salvaged from the house that formerly occupied the site serves as a portal to the new, and the wire gate is an abstract artwork. A chain-link fence along the sidewalk is a clue to the authorship of this sharp-edged ensemble.

Frank and Berta Gehry entrusted the design of their new residence to Sam, their elder son, and it has, inevitably, been compared to the transgressive house the father built more than 40 years earlier. That radical remodel of a modest Dutch Colonial house (1978) is a three-dimensional collage of plywood, chain-link and sheet metal, as provocative as a Robert Rauschenberg combine, which thrilled the avant-garde and outraged the neighbors. It confirmed Gehry's position as the most original and creative architect of the late-twentieth century, though it proved a handicap in winning establishment support for his masterpiece, Walt Disney Concert Hall.

ENGAGING NATURE

Sam grew up in that house and studied architecture before joining his father's office in 2007. He demonstrated his talent as lead designer on the 2008 Serpentine Pavilion in London's Kensington Gardens; a short-lived installation that was disassembled and found a new role as a music pavilion at Château La Coste, an arts park in the south of France. Its massive timber frame and canted panels of glass had a wild exuberance that has been disciplined in their latest incarnation. The frame of 12-by-12-inch (30.5 by 30.5 cm) Douglas fir beams within the two glass wings—dining to the left of the entry, living to the right— has the grandeur of a classical temple combined with the simplicity of a primitive post-and-beam hut. It also evokes a forest and imparts a sense of warmth and intimacy to these soaring volumes.

CALIFORNIA HOUSES

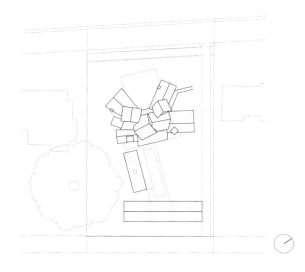

All the millwork, including a balcony looking down from the primary suite on the upper floor, is rotary-cut Douglas fir with a grain as bold as the patterned marbles Adolf Loos employed. But it is the same humble, knotted wood that the father used when he was a self-proclaimed "cheapskate architect." The Douglas fir table seats 20 and served as a work surface during the Covid exodus from the architect's office. The whole family was involved in the interior design of the house: Berta Gehry specified the vibrantly patterned tile floor in the kitchen, Sam designed cushioned seating, his wife, Joyce, conceived the rugs, and the father's colorful scaled fish have extended their fins and flown into the rafters. As Sam explains, "Frank was very involved in the planning, but he gave me a free hand on the aesthetics. We wanted to build a courtyard house in the Spanish tradition."

The dining room is slightly elevated to capture a glimpse of the canyon and ocean, but most of the vistas are inward looking. The living room is set down a couple of feet to engage the trees, casting their shadows across the white mesh blinds that screen the glass. The concrete floor incorporates radiant heating and is overlaid with bricks in a herringbone pattern. A casual family room to the rear looks out to the landscaped courtyard with its lap pool and pergola linking the 5,000-square-foot (464.5 m²) house to a rear wing of comparable size. There, Frank and Berta indulge their passion for classical music in an acoustically tuned room that has hosted some of the world's leading performers. Michael Eisner, a long-time friend and client gifted a Steinway grand piano, custom lacquered in Gehry's preferred shade of green.

To either side are two-floor blocks with guest rooms for visiting artists. Rooftop solar panels and nine geothermal wells provide much of the power, and clerestories open to draw ocean breezes into both halves of the house. Laurie Olin's landscaping conceals the houses to either side, but one neighbor looms over the courtyard: a magnificent Moreton Bay fig tree, planted by one of the earliest settlers more than a century ago.

Pebble Beach House
Monterey County

JIM JENNINGS ARCHITECTURE

Waves crash on a rocky shore studded with wind-torn cypresses along the scenic 17-Mile Drive that encircles Monterey Peninsula. Residents guard the natural beauty as vigilantly as they cling to traditional styles of building, for Monterey was the Spanish capital of Alta California as far back as 1776. Jim Jennings secured approval for one of the first modern houses near the picturesque village of Carmel in 2015 and was invited to replicate this feat in the small community of Pebble Beach. The clients were Stephen Ackley, cofounder of an upscale San Francisco real-estate company, and his wife Maryan, an accountant. They shared Jennings's minimalist aesthetic, along with his love of simplicity and openness. Luckily, a key member of the local architectural review board lent her support. "At last, a modern building," she exclaimed when the architect made his first presentation, and the board approved the design.

The narrow site is located a block from the ocean, and the clients wanted a compact four-bedroom house to accommodate their family, display their collection of contemporary art, and entertain friends. To provide breathing room, it was set back behind trees that conceal neighboring properties. The architect produced sketches that morphed into a three-floor, 6,700-square-foot (622.5 m²) house rooted among Andrea Cochran's plantings of olive, boxwood, and Japanese maples, as well as four reflecting pools. Irregular massing of the two upper levels makes the house appear smaller than it is, and one floor is underground, naturally lit from a skylight along the southeast side of the linear structure. Three rough-textured concrete walls enclose bedroom terraces on the opposite side. The house requires little power to warm, employing radiant heating in the stone floors, and a high-velocity, micro-duct system for cooling. There is a continuous envelope of insulation around the building, and the stone provides a heat sink that evens out changes in temperature.

Ackley brought his experience in building upscale houses to his meetings with the architect as they considered multiple choices of cladding materials. The concrete was poured in forms lined with 3-inch (7.6 cm) cedar boards to give the free-standing walls a refined character, and the exterior of the house was clad in a rainscreen of Pietra Serena sandstone on a 24-inch (61 cm) module and rectilinear panels of aluminum with a high-tech coating that preserves the silvery metal from the corrosion of salt air. The two materials were closely matched in tone, and the grids complement each other, their geometry animating blank walls that have an affinity with the minimalist sculptures of Donald Judd and Carl Andre. Only the garage door folds up, disrupting the aluminum grid. Warm gray surfaces lighten the steel-framed structure, interacting with shifts of light and evoking a ghost ship when the sea mists drift ashore.

ENGAGING NATURE

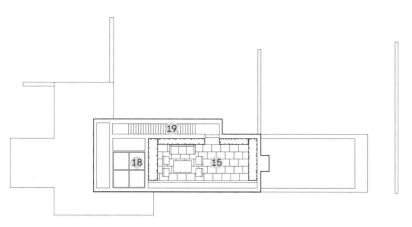

ROOF PLAN

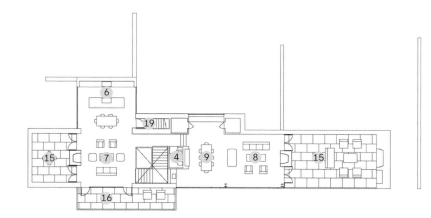

SECOND-FLOOR PLAN

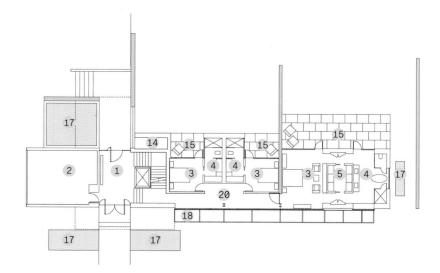

FIRST-FLOOR PLAN

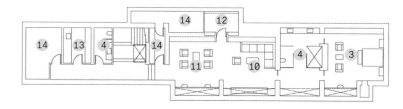

BASEMENT PLAN

1   Entry
2   Garage
3   Bedroom
4   Bathroom
5   Dressing room
6   Kitchen
7   Family area
8   Living area
9   Dining area
10   Media room
11   Lounge
12   Wine room
13   Laundry
14   Utility
15   Terrace
16   Balcony
17   Water
18   Skylight
19   Stairs to roof
20   Gallery

CALIFORNIA HOUSES

You enter the house on the first floor, where a gallery gives access to two bedrooms and the main suite. A staircase with cantilevered wood treads links the three floors and wraps around a skylit tower of translucent glass. Jennings calls this pillar of light the hinge of the house. Another flight of steps ascends from the top floor to a roof terrace, which offers sweeping views. A fourth bedroom, media room, wine store, and utilities occupy the basement.

On the second floor the family area and kitchen open onto a terrace, and rift-cut walnut cabinetry divides this space from the living area, which leads into a high-walled outdoor room at the far end. Zimbabwe black granite, lightened to emphasize its white markings, is employed on the terraces, and all the floors are clad in pale gray limestone. It is here, in the living areas, that you can best appreciate the free flow of space, the restrained décor by Leverone Design, and the oasis of calm the house provides to busy professionals when they leave their primary residence in Palo Alto to spend weekends in this refined work of art.

ENGAGING NATURE

CALIFORNIA HOUSES

ENGAGING NATURE

Wave House
Malibu

MARK DZIEWULSKI ARCHITECT

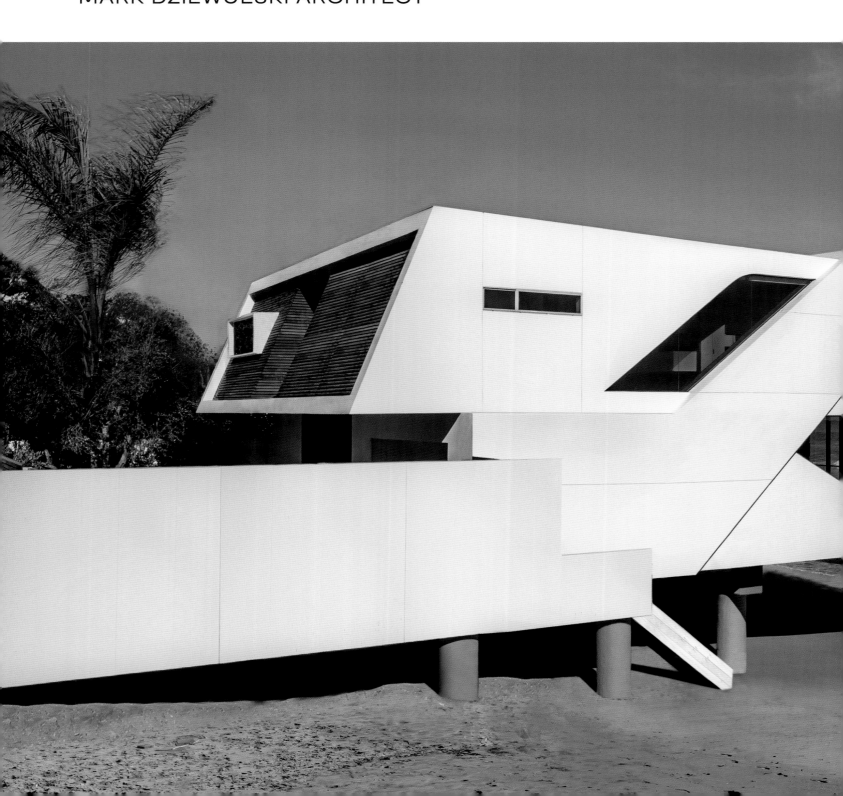

The combination of a great site and a generous client allows an architect to spread their wings and soar. Mark Dziewulski, a British-born architect with a peripatetic practice, made his reputation with such a project in Sacramento: a graceful lakeside pavilion that enhances its bucolic site. Fortune smiled again in Malibu, where a real-estate developer from St. Louis commissioned him to build a second home on the beach and encouraged him to take full advantage of the exposed lot. The challenge was to radically remodel an existing house, staying within its footprint and recycling the concrete piers that lofted it above the surf.

"I spent a lot of time sketching on the site, and then explored different options in the computer models, playing with the shapes until it felt right,"

explains the architect. "It had to be quite sculptural since it was exposed on one side and in front to the coast highway, where it would be seen by 50,000 drivers a day." Most houses on this coastal strip cram as much square footage as possible into an inert box dressed up as a Cape Cod, a classical palazzo, or a Tudor cottage. Here, Dziewulski has abstracted marine references to create a dynamic composition that leans forward to the ocean with decks cantilevered over the waves, and a diagonal bar that evokes a crane.

The steel-framed structure is faced in white cement plaster, and the entry façade is clad in moveable louvers of ipe wood. There is a two-car garage and guest parking in the walled forecourt that protects the compact, 3,200-square-foot (297.3 m²) house from the roar of traffic on the Pacific Coast Highway. Everything is elegantly composed, and the sharp corners of the exposed windows are curved to soften the angularity of the side façade. Crisp, springy, and gleaming white: it is a model of what a beach house should be.

The light and airy interior has the same elegant simplicity as the façades. An open staircase with a flanking wall of rough-textured stone rises through a central void, bathed in light from roof openings. That meets the biggest challenge of building on the ocean: balancing the glare off the water so that the landward side does not appear dark and cave-like. Kitchen, dining, and living areas are arranged in an L that wraps around the staircase. Glass sliders open onto a glass-balustraded deck that runs the full width of the house, creating a spacious platform for entertaining.

← FIRST-FLOOR PLAN

↓ SECOND-FLOOR PLAN

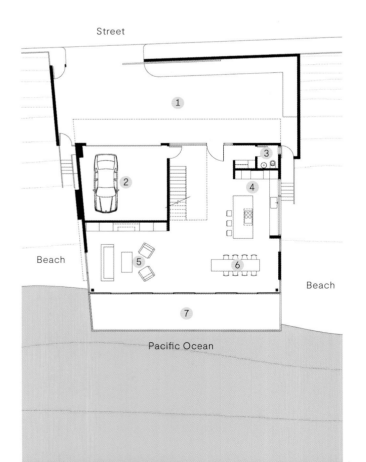

1   Entry court
2   Garage
3   WC
4   Kitchen
5   Living area
6   Dining area
7   Terrace
8   Primary closet
9   Primary bathroom
10 Primary bedroom
11 Guest bedroom
12 Bathroom

Jennice Tronciale of Tronciale Design created the spare interiors with assistance from Chimera Interiors. She made an inspired selection of contemporary classics that include seating by B&B Italia and Jasper Morrison in the living area, an oval dining table and glove chairs by Molteni, and custom, white-lacquered kitchen cabinetry from Italy. On the second floor, the primary suite is located to one side of the staircase, with two guest bedrooms on the other. The main bathroom has figured white marble walls and floors of honed Basaltina stone.

"God is in the details," declared Ludwig Mies van der Rohe, and Dziewulski has thought through every aspect of the house to make it inspirational and sustainable. Window openings are strategically placed to frame views of the ocean and up the coast while shutting out the road. The two second-floor balconies shade the lower deck from summer sun. The house is solidly rooted to withstand storms, and the anodized aluminum glazing bars resist the salt air without corroding. Best of all, the interior spaces have the liquid flow of the ocean that eddies just below.

ENGAGING NATURE

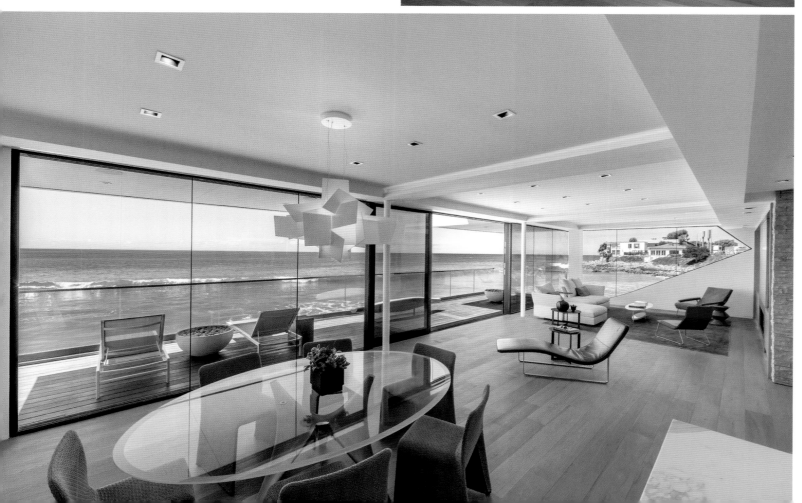

ENGAGING NATURE

Vault House
Oxnard

JOHNSTON MARKLEE

A long white block hovers over the sandy beach of Oxnard, 30 miles (48 km) northwest of Los Angeles. It shares a narrow ocean frontage with a tightly serried row of vacation houses, but the site to the south has yet to be developed, so this new addition stands out from its generic neighbors. U-shaped cuts in the seamless white façades frame glass and openings, as well as a deeply recessed terrace looking out to the surf. The Vault House has a steel-reinforced wood-frame structure, with a sprayed-on skin of GrailCoat, forming an elastomeric membrane that requires no expansion joints and should withstand the corrosive sea air. Scale-less and enigmatic, it looks as though a sculptor has carved a solid block of stone, and there is little sense of what it contains.

The program was simple. An LA-based couple with a taste for simplicity wanted a weekend escape where they could commune with nature, by themselves or with friends and their two grown daughters. The challenge was to create a sense of spaciousness on a skinny, tightly confined lot, and pull in natural light and views to every room. It is a test most California beach houses fail. They feel imprisoned by the public arena in front, a heavily trafficked coast road behind, and the houses that press in to either side. All too often, the house is designed in period style with clapboarded gables or a red-tiled roof, and this traditional symmetry inhibits the freedom to rethink the interiors. Mark Lee, Sharon Johnston, and their design team searched for a better solution, one that would turn the constraints to advantage.

They were required to raise the house 8 feet (2.4 m) above the ground to protect it from major storms or even a tsunami. The garage to the rear has walls that would readily collapse and allow a surge of water to flow under the concrete deck, which is supported on 38 piles and forms a solid foundation. The elevation provides security and imparts a sense of lightness to the block, as do the cut-outs. These are strategically placed to frame oblique views out and to filter light from above, and their asymmetry turns the long blank façades into abstract relief compositions. The owners' property line extends to the high-tide mark and, though the public has full access to the sand, the architects were permitted to extend the house 10 feet (3 m) beyond their nearest neighbor. That adds side views, turning a single framed prospect into a wrap-around panorama.

CALIFORNIA HOUSES

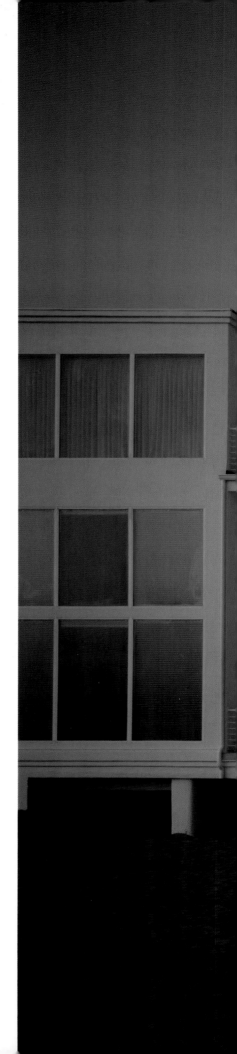

The big move was to divide the house in two by inserting a central courtyard that doubles as a patio sheltered from cool breezes and as a light well. The split-level section of the house offers glimpses of the ocean from the primary bedroom, set back behind the double-height living room, the kitchen–dining area below, and the rooms to the rear of the courtyard. Throughout the house, light enters from two or more points, balancing and diffusing the dazzle of sunlight reflected off water. Project architect Katrin Terstegen has written about the delayed "Wow!" that this house offers as you move from the enigmatic façade to the complexity of the interior, comparing it to the Villa Müller (1930) of Adolf Loos. Few modern houses offer such a dramatic transition.

You enter the Vault House from the narrow passage on the north side, and a flight of steps leads straight up to the courtyard, continuing on to the primary bedroom and roof terrace. From this enclosed, austere access route you progress from an outdoor room, through the low-ceilinged kitchen and into the lofty living room, which opens through sliders onto the sheltered terrace and the infinity of sky and ocean. There is a compelling sequence of arched ceiling vaults and, at every point, another vista beckons, above or to one side, enriching the spatial experience. It is a lively architectural promenade that complements the natural beauty of the site.

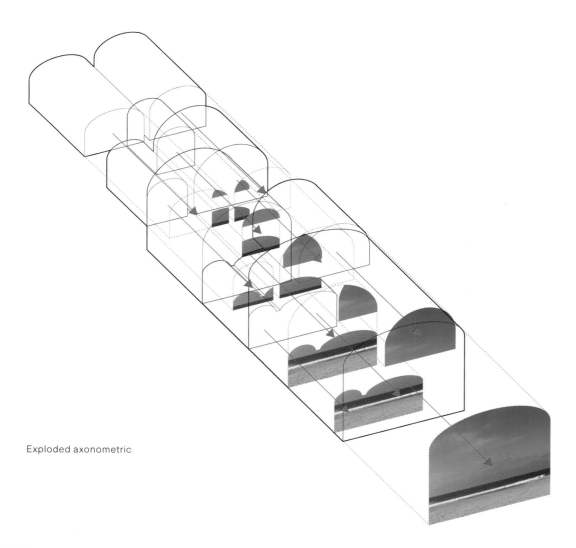

Exploded axonometric

CALIFORNIA HOUSES

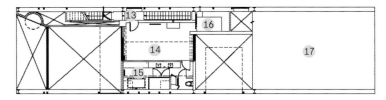

SECOND-FLOOR PLAN

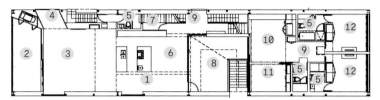

FIRST-FLOOR / SPLIT-LEVEL PLAN

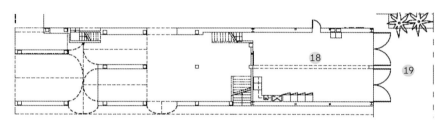

GARAGE PLAN

1   Entry / hallway
2   Deck
3   Living area
4   Alcove
5   Bathroom
6   Kitchen / dining area
7   Pantry
8   Courtyard
9   Hallway
10 Multi-purpose room
11 Library
12 Bedroom
13 Stairs
14 Primary bedroom
15 Primary bathroom
16 Primary closet
17 Split level
18 Garage
19 Driveway

CALIFORNIA HOUSES

Ocean-Front Retreat

MICHAEL MALTZAN ARCHITECTURE

Michael Maltzan has won acclaim for architecture that shows art to best advantage, the humanity of his housing for the homeless, and the dynamic Sixth Street Bridge, a new landmark in downtown Los Angeles. Less familiar are the houses he has tailored to the demands of artists and collectors. These display his special gift for creating forms and spaces that engage the senses while enhancing the spirit of place.

Commissioned by a patron of art and architecture to create a retreat for family and friends on an expansive site beside the ocean, he took a fresh approach. A low, enigmatic façade conceals the 10,700 square feet (994 m²) of enclosed space from the street. The upper level is raised on columns so that it appears to float above the sand, opening up vistas of the ocean from the four ground-level guest suites to the rear of the site. The house is tapered on plan to accommodate a pool on one side, a basketball court on the other, and a shady undercroft for summer gatherings in between. That gives it a sculptural quality and blurs the boundary between indoors and outdoors. California has a long tradition of houses that enclose a courtyard; here the courtyard envelops the house.

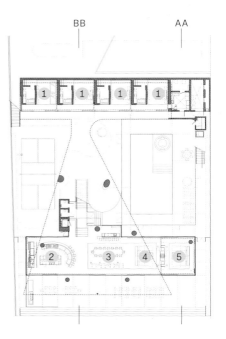

FIRST-FLOOR PLAN

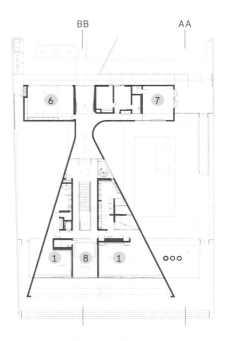

SECOND-FLOOR PLAN

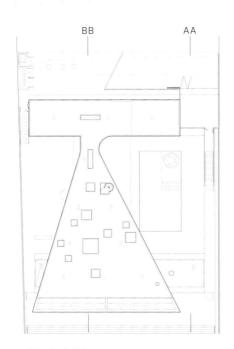

ROOF PLAN

1   Bedroom
2   Kitchen
3   Dining area
4   Living area
5   Den
6   Garage
7   Gym
8   Sitting room

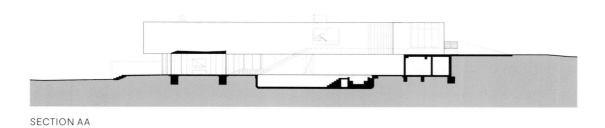

SECTION AA

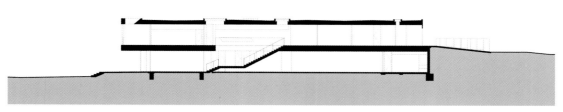

SECTION BB

CALIFORNIA HOUSES

As Maltzan explains, "It's important that the singular view of the ocean does not dominate every moment of your life. There are multiple ways of moving and seeing, with views out to the side in unexpected places. Viewers should create their own narratives, otherwise the house becomes overly controlling."

The wedge of the upper floor hovers above the ground. One of the columns is inclined to impart a sense of motion and a staircase descends in a graceful arc. A cut-out frames a spiral stair leading up to the roof. Its treads are echoed in a composition of black and white stripes, both bathed in rippling reflections off the pool. The house is open and transparent, but the windowless façade is punctuated only by a square of reflective glass and a recessed portal. That gives it the slightly surreal quality of David Hockney's *A Bigger Splash* (1967) and heightens the drama of entry. You step through the narrow opening into a skylit concourse and are drawn forward by a glimpse of the ocean. In the middle of the concourse is the staircase that descends to the living areas. These lead out through pocketing sliders to the pool and to sand dunes that partially screen the public beach. To the right is an open kitchen with a counter for casual dining, to the left a long dining table flanked by Arne Jacobsen side chairs, and, at the far end, a compact media room.

ENGAGING NATURE

CALIFORNIA HOUSES

The owner realized that a beach house exposed to sun, humidity, and salt air was no place for his collection of contemporary art. Instead, he acquired various wall drawings from the estate of Sol LeWitt, an artist whose bold geometries he greatly admired. Angled lines and concentric circles of black were applied to white plaster by one of the artist's teams, creating a dazzling succession of murals that animate the entry portal, the concourse, and the stairway to the roof. Another suite of drawings in subtle colors enliven a study and the downstairs guest rooms. These artworks are designed to withstand the elements and can be repainted if they ever fade. They complement the sweep of the architecture and recall the murals in Roman houses, Renaissance villas, and Baroque palaces.

The house is a fusion of art, architecture, and nature; an immersive experience that enlarges your field of vision. At the same time, it offers a relaxed setting for family gatherings and a sense of intimacy when the owners are home alone. The refinement of the primary suites contrasts with the unpretentious character of public spaces that flow into each other and embrace the natural features of the site. This is a house that is big-boned but not excessive, in which a few basic features have a generosity of proportion.

Roofless House
Atherton

CRAIG STEELY ARCHITECTURE

Conveniently located between San Francisco and Silicon Valley, Atherton is the wealthiest small city in America and residents are determined to maintain its exclusivity. Heritage trees are valued over people unless they are tech millionaires building on a minimum lot size of an acre. Craig Steely was commissioned to design a new house at the end of a cul-de-sac. It was surrounded by mature trees, but backed up to the blank rear walls of several neighbors. The client was an executive who had grown up in Venezuela and wanted a sanctuary in which she could spend much of the time outdoors, taking advantage of the Mediterranean climate. She had owned the land for 10 years, wondering how to build on it, and she chose Steely for his focus on open space in the houses he had designed in Hawaii and northern California.

On his second visit to the site, Steely proposed a simple sequence of rooms opening onto three spacious courtyards, surrounded entirely by a high fence that would block the dismal urban vista and direct the eye upward to the tree canopy and sky. The owner was familiar with courtyard houses from her homeland and welcomed the security and privacy this scheme would provide. The rectangle of enclosed space is rounded in places to steer around trees and mark the principal point of entry, giving the plan a faint resemblance to one of Henry Moore's reclining figures. A detached garage is linked to the house by a canopied breezeway, and one expansive window flanks the pivoting entry door on the north side.

What makes the house such a popular addition to the community is the landscaping of wild grasses and newly planted birch trees that envelop the 14-foot-high (4.3 m) cedar fence. Most of the neighbors are walled off at the boundary line and there are no sidewalks in Atherton; here, a sliver of parkland mediates between road and house. The fence becomes an object in the landscape, an expanse of weathered wood with sensuous curves that make it a congenial foil to the trees. Many new arrivals strive for effect, maxing out their sites and mimicking historical styles, with the occasional contemporary mansion. And, since they are entirely concealed from everyone but the owner, they add nothing to the townscape. By contrast, this house is an organic canvas dappled with shadows and naturally weathered. It is timeless and modest in scale, enigmatic in its windowless façades but entirely at home in its leafy setting.

ENGAGING NATURE

The Roofless House is probably one of the smallest in town: half the 5,000 square feet (464.5 m²) within the fence is uncovered. That pulls in abundant natural light and cool breezes, and each interior space opens through glass sliders onto one of the tree-shaded courtyards. These offer some of the intensity of a James Turrell Skyspace, focusing the gaze upward where the movement of leaves and branches complements that of passing clouds and you are constantly aware of shifts in light and weather. The sky becomes a fifth façade, and the wood—a more refined cut of cedar for the inner walls and cabinetry—is a tactile, aromatic presence. The expanses of glass reveal internal vistas from the living areas at one end to the primary suite and a second guest bedroom at the other. These orthogonal indoor and outdoor rooms play off the curvilinear elements in the fence.

There is no design review board in Atherton—wealth and invisibility confer freedom on residents—and Steely's proposal was respectful of the trees, so this unconventional scheme was quickly approved and provoked no opposition. He understood that the idea of shutting yourself off from the world might seem intimidating, so he made sketches and a succession of cut-away models to explain it to his client. And she shared his preference for a compact house that would eliminate the boundaries between indoors and out.

CALIFORNIA HOUSES

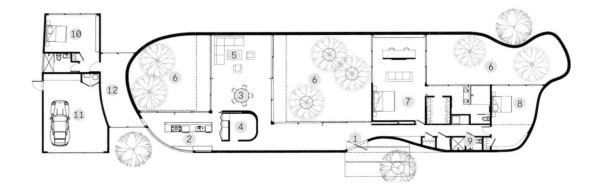

1   Entry
2   Kitchen
3   Dining
4   Pantry
5   Living room
6   Courtyard
7   Primary bedroom suite
8   Bedroom
9   Bathroom
10 Guest Suite
11 Garage
12 Breezeway

ENGAGING NATURE

Branch House Montecito

PETER TOLKIN + SARAH LORENZEN
ARCHITECTURE (TOLO)

As Montecito was built up, many of the evergreen coast live oaks that once covered the land were cleared, and they are now a protected species. That posed a challenge for TOLO, who was commissioned by an art-loving couple to insert a house into a grove of oaks. She is an eighth-generation Californian, a dancer who later became a painter. He grew up in a farming town in Ohio and founded a successful manufacturing company. The wife wanted a house that would accommodate their collection of contemporary art and allow them to commune with nature—a radical shift from their century-old Spanish-style residence in Pasadena.

ENGAGING NATURE

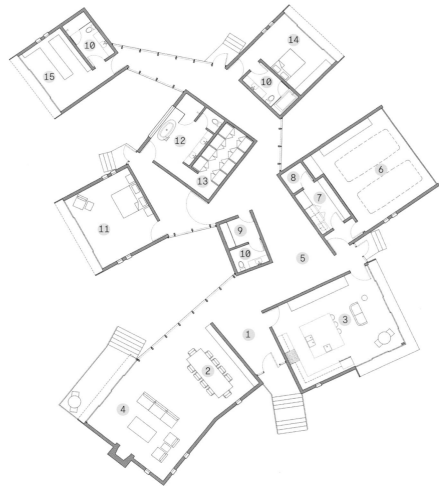

1   Foyer
2   Dining area
3   Kitchen
4   Living area
5   Gallery
6   Garage
7   Laundry
8   Mechanical room
9   Powder room
10 Bathroom
11 Primary bedroom
12 Primary bathroom
13 Primary closet
14 Bedroom
15 Office

CALIFORNIA HOUSES

They bought a ranch house in Montecito for the beauty of the one-acre site, even though the dwelling was badly sited and too cramped to display large canvases. Rather than remodeling this generic structure, Peter Tolkin persuaded them to replace it with a house that comprises separate pavilions linked by galleries and raised on concrete piles to avoid damaging the tree roots. That restores the ground plane to wildlife and allows rainwater to return to the land, rather than channeling it from a paved forecourt into storm drains as the old house did. Wade Graham Landscape Studio planted new oaks and drought-resistant native plants, varying the mix with succulents and introducing ferns along the creek that meanders through the property.

In a succession of models, Tolkin sought an ideal configuration for the 4,700-square-foot (436.6 m²) house and detached painting pavilion. As built, it performs a graceful dance, circling the trees but never stepping on their feet. The timber-frame structure is clad in copper shingles to protect it from the wildfires that are becoming ever-more frequent and destructive, and this armor-plating projects out to shield the windows from direct sun and falling branches. The copper is acquiring a patina that allows it to merge into the landscape. Rooftop solar panels generate most of the power.

CALIFORNIA HOUSES

It is instructive to compare this house with those of Australian architect Glenn Murcutt, whose rural dwellings "sit lightly on the land" (to use his favorite phrase) and employ humble materials that are meticulously detailed. TOLO is equally fond of unpretentious, off-the-shelf materials and deceptively simple forms, and the interior suggests a collaboration between early Frank Gehry and Carlo Scarpa, the Italian master of detail. The raw elements express the owners' passion for contemporary art—as in an artist's loft. The galvanized metal handrails, concrete floor and plywood cabinetry are complemented by the exposed structural frame of Douglas fir. In contrast, the kitchen and two bathrooms are lit from soaring roof lanterns and are clad entirely in glazed clay tiles from Heath Ceramics. The expanse of bold color in each enhances their spatial qualities.

The major rooms can be closed off by room-height oak doors and the windows act like camera lenses framing distinctive compositions. The galleries that link them have high-performance glass on one side to filter UV, and white drywall on the other for the display of artworks. In a classic country house, you feel as though you are the center of the world, with axial views radiating out. That concept, born in the Renaissance and refined in later centuries, has been fragmented. Here, you feel calm and protected in each of the pavilions, while the galleries accentuate the sense of motion. As with the materiality of the house, this alternation enriches the experience of moving from one room to the next.

The careful planning might easily have come to naught. "Many of my best clients have been women," says Tolkin, "and it was the wife who empowered us to take risks on this project. Her husband passed before construction began but she decided to move ahead and make it a creative act that would serve his memory."

ENGAGING NATURE

CALIFORNIA HOUSES

ENGAGING NATURE

Cube House
Mill Valley

KOJI TSUTSUI ARCHITECT & ASSOCIATES

Mill Valley is an affluent town in Marin County that has retained its rural character and adjoins a preserve of old-growth redwoods. An architect who had worked with Louis Kahn sold a steep wooded slope that was part of his property to Koji Tsutsui and dared him: "Now you try building there!" Tsutsui, who has an architectural practice in the city and in Tokyo, accepted the challenge, and designed a cluster of 10 interconnected cubes that cascade down the hillside. They are raised into the tree canopy on deeply embedded, galvanized-steel columns that protect them from mudslides and allow wildlife to pass below. The wood-frame units rest on concrete pads and are clad in a rainscreen of cement boards. Deer shelter underneath in bad weather.

Working with a limited budget, the architect had to use basic materials and specify elements that could be hand-carried to the site and assembled without cranes or heavy equipment. "The design was inspired by a school I designed in Uganda, creating a village-like cluster of small units to break up the mass," Tsutsui explains. "My grandfather was a carpenter who designed tree houses and I may have inherited his love of craft. I thought that fragmentation would make it easy to build but it proved harder and costlier than I had anticipated."

Each module is set at a 22.5-degree angle to the next and together they form a figure 8 on plan, enclosing two tiny courtyards. These serve as points of entry from the long flight of steps that links the 1,700-square-foot (158 m²) house to a carport at the upper level and another street below. From top to bottom, the structure is as tall as a conventional two-floor house. Inside the upper entry, two bedrooms and a bathroom are fully enclosed, and you step down to the living areas, study, kitchen, and a roof deck, which open into each other from side to side with a shift of level between. Tsutsui hates rooms that are completely walled off and here, in the living areas, he has achieved a free flow of space and constant shifts of perspective. He likens it to the flow of blood through the human body, and it fosters a feeling of sociability between the owners and their guests.

ENGAGING NATURE

Traditional Japanese houses, with their simple post-and-beam construction, and lightweight sliding screens that open one room to another and to a covered veranda, helped shape the work of Frank Lloyd Wright and successive generations of American architects, especially on the West Coast. You can see their influence in the Case Study Houses of southern California. The Japanese came late to Modernism, but in recent decades, they have played extraordinary variations on basic themes, fusing the traditions and innovations of East and West. Cube House is a perfect fit for its site, in its respect for the land, and the way its large windows frame the trees, while evoking the spatial complexity and tight-knit planning of the Japanese avant-garde.

Each pod is minimal; the drywall and painted plywood floors are impeccably finished, and the house has the character of an intricate cabinet. Tsutsui gave up the house when he moved back to Tokyo for several years to take on a major commission and he feared that its spartan interior might be off-putting to an American. But the house has found new and appreciative owners. For Mark Funke, a rare book dealer with a store in Mill Valley, and his wife, graphic designer Joanna Funke, it is a welcoming oasis. Trees screen out neighboring houses and provide the calming presence of nature a half-hour drive from the Golden Gate Bridge. Carrying armloads of books up and down the steps, and the need to clear leaves from the rooftop drains several times a year are Funke's only reservations.

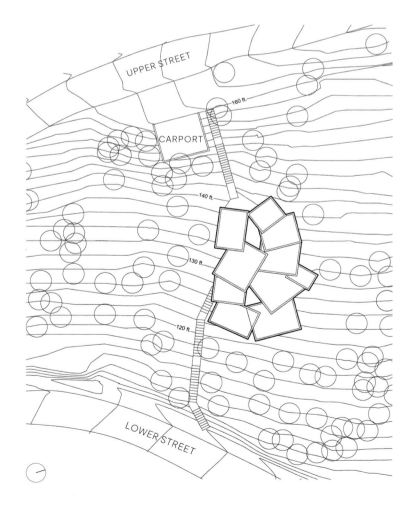

ENGAGING NATURE

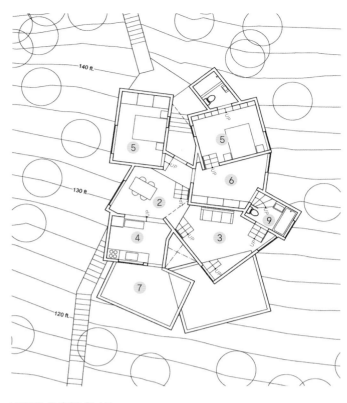

UPPER-FLOOR PLAN

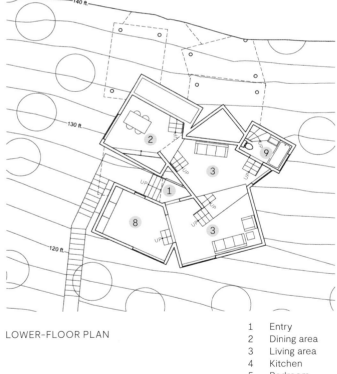

LOWER-FLOOR PLAN

1 Entry
2 Dining area
3 Living area
4 Kitchen
5 Bedroom
6 Dressing room
7 Roof deck
8 Study / bedroom
9 Bathroom

ENGAGING NATURE

Forest House
Mendocino County

ENVELOPE A+D

"The woods are lovely, dark, and deep," wrote poet Robert Frost, and parts of northern California preserve some of the wild beauty that greeted the first settlers. A family who live in the San Francisco Bay Area and like to go camping bought 40 acres of old-growth madrone, manzanita, and live oak in Mendocino County, a three-hour drive from the city. They intended to pitch their tents there, but the estate is home to a pack of 300-pound (136 kg) wild boars that defend their territory aggressively, so they invited Douglas Burnham to design a structure that would raise them above the ground and deepen their immersion in the sights and sounds of the forest. He knew his clients well, having previously designed five projects for the family, and accepted the commission enthusiastically.

It started with a single platform and evolved into a group of four hybrid tent-cabins constructed from stained cedar boards with inclined roofs of high-performance fabric. They are raised on stilts and located in open spaces between trees, taking advantage of shifts in the ground level. There is one for the parents, another for guests, and a two-part cabin with bunk beds for the children and their friends, linked by redwood walkways to a communal cabin with a kitchen and terrace. So thick is the forest that it conceals each of these structures from the others even though they are physically close, and it provides welcome shade in the extreme heat of summer. The property backs up to land that is preserved in its pristine state by a private trust, ensuring that the complex is likely to retain its isolation.

The guest cabin was built first, as a prototype that architect and clients could critique. As Burnham explains, "we had reviewed the design with them in models and discussions but, because they were long-time clients and there was a high level of trust, we told them: 'this is an experiment; we are taking risks with you, playing with ideas we are just discovering, so let's make a few adjustments.' We fully enclosed the interior, adding bronzed glass for privacy and allowing the owners to hang art on the walls, but you could hear the rain and the wind in the trees through the roof." A small crew built the remaining structures, one at a time, without any use of heavy equipment that would have damaged trees. It is uncomfortably cold and wet in winter, so the family wait for spring to go there for weekends or even a month at a time.

1   Bunk cabin
2   Guest cabin
3   Communal cabins
4   Parents' cabin / bathroom

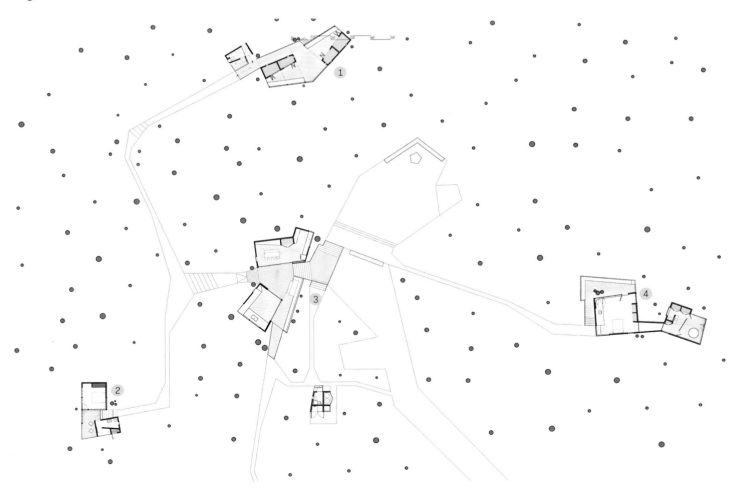

ENGAGING NATURE

CALIFORNIA HOUSES

The black cabins with their dark-green roofs fade into the shadows and the glass mirrors the forest. Wood stilts are enclosed by stainless-steel tubes as they enter drilled piers at ground level. Interiors are meticulously crafted with exposed framing of natural cedar, light-stained cedar floors, and Douglas fir plywood walls. Rooms open to decks through pocketing glass sliders, with retractable mesh screens to exclude mosquitos. The one-way glass in the bathrooms ensures that you are constantly at one with nature, seeming to float between canopy and floor. All the showers are outdoor with optional curtains, so that you start your day in the open air.

A photovoltaic array covers most of the power needs, and cross ventilation provides natural cooling. There is a well and storage tank, as well as a swimming pool that would serve as a refuge if the family were trapped by a wildfire, but there seemed no point in armoring the structures. Burnham explains that a forest fire is so hot it would melt any protective cladding, and it is unlikely that emergency crews would reach such a remote property in time to save it. The owners decided to accept the risk.

ENGAGING NATURE

Weekend Cabin
Yucca Valley

ORA ARCHITECTURE & DESIGN

1   Entry
2   Kitchen
3   Living / dining area
4   Primary bedroom
5   Primary bathroom
6   Bedroom
7   Bathroom
8   Living / dining / bedroom area
9   Deck
10 Patio
11 Parking

CALIFORNIA HOUSES

ENGAGING NATURE

The sun–baked wilderness beyond Palm Springs, with its dramatic rock formations, is the polar opposite of the soft green landscape around Waterford, the ancient Irish city where Oonagh Ryan grew up. She relocated to Los Angeles in 1994, struggled through the recession, and now has a flourishing practice. Her next-door neighbors, a couple who run political campaigns for progressive candidates, asked her to remodel a desert cabin they had bought as a weekend retreat. They were drawn to its lack of pretension and the way it was hidden away on a five-acre lot, bordering on federally protected land that guaranteed unspoiled views. But it had been built without a permit, and a local building inspector condemned it. It would have cost as much to bring it up to current codes as to build anew, so it was torn down. Ryan was tasked with designing a modern interpretation of the old without disturbing any of the rocks and trees.

Alison Morgan and Parke Skelton love the outdoors and they wanted
to share the natural beauty with their two grown children and
friends, without overwhelming the site. Ryan sited a three-bedroom,
1,200-square-foot (111.5 m²) cabin on the existing flat pad and added
a fourth bedroom atop a one-car garage, setting it apart and orienting
it in the opposite direction to assure privacy to both units. The dialogue
between the two volumes enriches the composition and may presage
a third cabin as another generation come to stay. The couple used this
auxiliary unit as their office during the pandemic, and the garage also
houses storage, a laundry, and their vintage teardrop camper that can
accommodate an extra guest. A second parking place was required,
and this is located beside the entry beneath a wood pergola that doubles
as a shady outside dining area.

ENGAGING NATURE

CALIFORNIA HOUSES

Although the house feels remote, the small town of Yucca Valley is only a 10-minute drive down a dirt road. The clients hired an experienced local contractor who did an exemplary job of pouring a concrete slab, polished to serve as the floor, erecting the wood frame, and cladding the studs with integrally colored stucco in a soft green that picks up on the trees. Every aspect of the design, from the pitched roofs to the mechanical services and septic tank, was driven by the tight budget and the need for durable, low-maintenance finishes. To protect it from the wildfires that sweep through this area, the roof was clad in corrugated metal, bronze-toned to harmonize with the rocks and extended out to shade windows from direct sun in summer. To mitigate heat loss and gain, insulation was pumped into the roof cavity. At an altitude of 3,200 feet (975.4 m), breezes cool the interior and solar panels should reduce energy consumption to near zero.

The design of the exterior went through multiple iterations as playful elements were simplified, and the interior was meticulously planned to achieve the highest quality at the lowest cost. Ryan used standard windows and doors, but specified high-performance glass. The windows are placed to frame the most interesting rock formations, and the first thing the couple see as they wake is a pyramidal pile called Big Daddy. They have brought an heirloom gas stove, adapting it to operate from a propane tank. The Heath Ceramics tiles they coveted for the bathrooms and kitchen seemed too costly, but they were able to acquire inexpensive seconds from the factory, challenging the architects to deploy six sizes in twenty-seven different colors. Ikea cabinets are customized with birch-ply millwork. The furnishings are a nod to the owners' mid-century-modern house in LA.

Frugal yet impeccably detailed, this is a model response to family needs and the character of the site. In contrast to so much recent development, it enhances the rugged landscape. As Ryan observes, "We don't design for people with unlimited budgets, and we want to give our clients more than they expected."

ENGAGING NATURE

WEAVING THE URBAN FABRIC

Suburban tract housing has engulfed most established settlements in California, and it breeds conformity. Builders stick to a few profitable patterns, and neighbors become fixated on the status quo and oppose change, much as the body combats viruses. Upscale gated communities often impose rigid design guidelines to assure a uniformity of style—usually an ersatz historicism. The goal is to make these houses broadly appealing and easy to resell. The art of architecture has little place in such calculations.

Historic communities, from San Francisco to downtown Santa Barbara (rebuilt in Spanish style after the 1925 earthquake) are even more resistant to innovative forms. There is some justification for this defensiveness: a single overbearing structure can disrupt the harmony of a street of Craftsman bungalows or Art Deco villas. The challenge for architects is to find ways of standing out while fitting in, respecting the scale and spirit of the community without mimicking every detail. Sometimes the line-up is so eclectic that the boldest statement soon becomes part of the context.

The urban renewal programs of the 1960s, when whole neighborhoods were leveled and replaced by high-rise estates, have rightly been discredited. But the desire to preserve everything old has impeded new initiatives and the densification that would increase the supply of affordable housing. Ironically, the Mar Vista Tract of small white cubes that Gregory Ain built in the 1940s for factory workers in West Los Angeles was almost rejected for its radicalism but is now a treasured, high-priced enclave of urbanity. There is scant chance of realizing so idealistic a project today.

Hidden House
San Francisco

OGRYDZIAK PRILLINGER ARCHITECTS (OPA)

Telegraph Hill is quintessential San Francisco with its serried rows of wood-framed houses clinging to steep slopes. Rebuilt after the devastating fire and earthquake of 1906, it was initially an unpretentious, bohemian neighborhood. Since then, it has become what OPA, the partnership of Luke Ogrydziak and Zoë Prillinger, describe as "a place so in love with its history and charm that it strenuously resists contemporary development. Powerful neighborhood groups multiply the difficulties already imposed by the conservative San Francisco Planning Code, and effectively stall any project that fails to comply with their historicist vision of the city."

Those constraints prompted OPA to create an audacious 2,900-square-foot (269.4 m²) house concealed behind a cedar-wood rainscreen that incorporates an archetypal bay window. Pre-weathered slats are elegantly rotated to admit light through the bay while serving as a privacy screen and cut away in an elongated V to illuminate the staircase. Within the mandatory height limit of 38 feet (11.6 m) above grade are four floors, ranging from a sunken garage, guest apartment, and skylit art studio to a third-floor primary suite with terraces overlooking the city. Officially, it is a remodel of a decrepit bungalow, but the old building is no more than a ghost inhabiting the lower floors and walls. The new conforms to a zoning envelope that the city granted to an earlier, unrealized development, and was further reduced by the insistence of a neighbor that his view of the Golden Gate Bridge was sacrosanct.

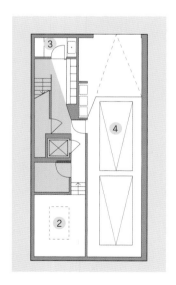

LOWER-FLOOR PLAN

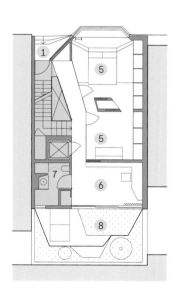

FIRST-FLOOR PLAN

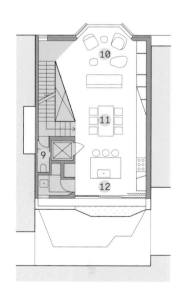

SECOND-FLOOR PLAN

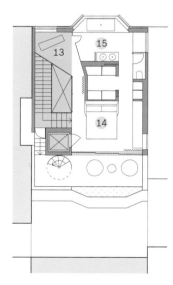

THIRD-FLOOR PLAN

CALIFORNIA HOUSES

1 Entry
2 Art studio
3 Utility
4 Garage
5 Bedroom
6 Office
7 Bathroom
8 Garden
9 Powder room
10 Living area
11 Dining area
12 Kitchen
13 Study
14 Primary bedroom
15 Primary bathroom

This was OPA's second design for the site. Doug Smith and Lorna Stevens, a sophisticated, well-traveled couple, put the first on hold following the 2008 recession. Four years later, Smith had launched a successful company and the couple had a larger budget, so they and the architects agreed to embark on a more ambitious design. Having grown up on the East Coast, worked in Germany, and raised their children in suburban Marin County, they wanted to participate in the cultural life of the city and find a living environment that was personal and expressive of the easy-going spirit of California.

To realize that vision, OPA split the house in two. A skylit staircase running up one side of the house became a vibrant steel sculpture creating a processional route from bottom to top. "I don't want to be minimal—that's boring," declared Stevens. "I want a color that brings me joy! Blue brings in the beautiful California sky." As an artist, she is sensitive to the nuances of color, and the couple spent a year deciding on the tone of the painted steel. This provides an immersive experience, complementing the neutral tones of the living areas and bedrooms with their concrete floors, ash millwork, and mesh screens that diffuse the LED strip lighting in the ceilings.

To preserve the neighbor's view, OPA crushed one section of the house, generating angular folds in the steel that wraps the staircase and imparts a kinetic energy to the space. The sharp geometries offer a radical contrast to the sensuously curved plaster interior that OPA created in Softie, a Modernist house overlooking San Francisco Bay. As Prillinger observes, "We're interested in pushing the limits of what architecture can do and investigating different languages. In the Hidden House we tried to avoid right angles and achieve a dynamic quality." That spirit is carried to edge of the confined 25-by-50-foot (7.6 by 15.2 m) site. To minimize the impact of a house that backs up to the shallow rear yard, they covered the blank wall with a dazzle pattern. The owner of this rental property was delighted to have a free paint job.

Behind its mask, Hidden House flows fluidly from one side to the other and vertically. The shift of tone and materiality makes it seem much larger and more complex than it is: a habitable work of art for the artist and entrepreneur who live there. And its compact footprint, abundant natural light, shading devices, and plantings make it a model of sustainability.

WEAVING THE URBAN FABRIC

OPA added a sensuously curved interior to Softie,
a remodeled house overlooking San Francisco Bay.

WEAVING THE URBAN FABRIC

Light Box
San Francisco

VEEV DESIGN

By day, the live—work space Raveevarn Choksombatchai built for herself presents itself to the street as a grid of perforated anodized–aluminum panels; a blank façade sandwiched between two neighboring buildings with nothing but a number to suggest the house that lies behind. It yields some of its secrets after dark when lighting reveals the outlines of furniture, a car in the garage, and a figure moving around. The architect grew up in Bangkok where latticework is widely employed for privacy and ventilation, as it is in Islamic countries. She wanted to use 3D printing to customize her screen but that proved too costly, so she ordered manufactured sheets with small and larger holes. These are attached to channel supports and overlaid in places to create a moiré effect. Floor-to-ceiling glazing with operable openings for ventilation is set back from the screen. Custom aluminum shelving inside the glass provides another layer of visual interference.

The simplicity of this 2,100-square-foot (195 m²) cube belies its troubled birth and the subtleties of its interior. It is located in SOMA (south of Market Street), a light-industrial district that has drawn designers and start-ups, chic restaurants, and stores in growing numbers, but still has an edgy character. The architecture is mundane but still there are hurdles to clear before you can build anything. It took the architect three years to secure a demolition permit for a badly decayed house, and she had to pay two PhD students, a museum curator, and an engineer to produce a report attesting that the decrepit house on the site had no historical significance. Her proposal to develop the site as three residential units with first-floor retail won a Progressive Architecture Award, but she was unable to find a cooperative developer. She decided to create a more modest structure for herself and, to spare herself another ordeal with Planning, applied to the Building Department for a renovation permit. They approved, on condition she replace the foundations and walls, so it became a ground-up project.

WEAVING THE URBAN FABRIC

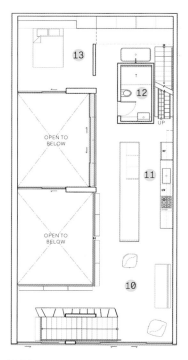

SECOND-FLOOR PLAN

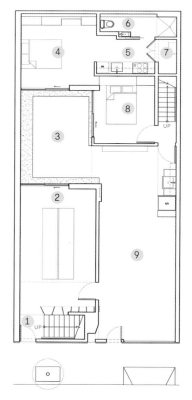

FIRST-FLOOR PLAN

CALIFORNIA HOUSES

There are three entries to: the garage, the house, and the courtyard.
Every room, including a rental unit to the rear, draws abundant natural
light from an inner courtyard, and the open plan adds to the sense
of spaciousness. A slender black steel column supports the upper floor
since the budget did not stretch to long-span beams. There is a feeling of
abstraction in the crisp, monochromatic décor: white walls and cabinetry,
concrete floors on the lower level, black-stained wood on the stair
treads and above. That makes the vibrant accents all the more powerful.
Choksombatchai grew up amid the brilliant tilework of Buddhist temples
and the saffron robes of monks, and it is easy to imagine the memories of
that heritage imprinting themselves on her subconscious. The garage and
the folded planes that conceal services at the entry to the courtyard are
painted saffron; the upstairs bathroom is wrapped in magenta and lined
with deep blue. The perforations of the aluminum screen are mimicked
in a blue tile mosaic, and other color accents recur through the house.

This is a house of layers, from the internal shear walls to the transparency
of the glass-enclosed bedroom and the translucent fabric around
the top of the bathroom that acts as another light box within the larger
volume. Shadows dapple the interior and the owner revels in the
choreography of materials that constitute her private domain, from
which she can work remotely with her home-based associates.
There is a double-height first-floor study, but the whole house adjusts
to varied patterns of use; the dining table, with its orange Eames side
chairs, doubles as a forum for informal meetings.

1   Entry
2   Study
3   Courtyard (open to sky)
4   Guest room
5   Kitchenette
6   Bathroom
7   Mechanical room
8   Bedroom
9   Garage
10 Living room
11 Kitchen / dining area
12 Primary bathroom
13 Primary bedroom

WEAVING THE URBAN FABRIC

CALIFORNIA HOUSES

Oakwood
San Francisco

STANLEY SAITOWITZ/
NATOMA ARCHITECTS

This is a third infill located in a quiet residential precinct of the district that grew up around the Mission Dolores. Movie buffs will remember its garden from a memorable scene in Alfred Hitchcock's *Vertigo* (1958). Mission Street is home to Hispanic immigrants, but other parts of the neighborhood have been gentrified by an influx of techies. That persuaded a developer to commission a 4,000-square-foot (371.6 m²) house on the site of a decaying 1920s residence.

The street is a mishmash of styles, dating back to the Victorian era, allowing the architect to design a new façade that is much bolder and more open than that of Hidden House (see p. 110). However, there is less to hide, for the interior is distinguished by its generous proportions and clean lines, laid out in an intelligent way to appeal to a broad swathe of buyers. For lack of a client, it has no quirky details: rather it serves, like the post-war Case Study Houses, as an exemplar of rational, contemporary design.

Stanley Saitowitz has been practicing in San Francisco for almost 50 years so he has a deep understanding of its urban grain and its architectural vernacular. The old house was set back behind the building line, which gave him the opportunity to add a concrete moment frame that provides lateral stability and abstracts the typical city façade. The proportions echo that of a bay window and the frame obviates the need for internal shear walls that would block light. Unabashedly modern, it captures the spirit of the city's traditional row houses in which the façades define what lies behind, and the parapet that bounds the top floor terrace evokes a cornice line. The architect calls it "contemporary Mission style," and it recalls the white concrete buildings that Irving Gill built in southern California a century ago.

The house extends the footprint of the reconstructed original, adds two floors, and is stepped back to the rear and sides to stay within the zoning envelope. At the back of the sunken garage is a side entrance to the house on the upper levels and an 800-square-foot (74.3 m²) apartment for guests or rental stepped down from the rear yard. A central, skylit staircase ascends to the living areas on the second floor, the primary suite and two bedrooms on the third, and a multi-purpose room at the top. There are rear terraces on all three of the upper floors and a front terrace on the fourth overlooking the city. Stairs and the service core divide the middle floors in two, and a light well illuminates the center and balances the light from the expansive glazing to front and rear.

FIRST-FLOOR PLAN   SECOND-FLOOR PLAN   THIRD-FLOOR PLAN   FOURTH-FLOOR PLAN

1   Entry
2   Garage
3   Bedroom
4   Living room
5   Fire place / TV
6   Kitchen
7   Dining area
8   Sitting area
9   Deck
10 Powder room
11 Bathroom
12 Closet
13 Office
14 Primary bedroom
15 Primary bathroom
16 Primary suite deck
17 Family room

CALIFORNIA HOUSES

CALIFORNIA HOUSES

Saitowitz is working with the same enlightened developer on a 32-unit
block in the city. Everything in the submission conformed to the
regulations, but it was mired in planning review for more than two years.
In the Sonoma County town of Healdsburg he had better luck.
Two friends who are land-use lawyers living in large country houses
decided to retire to Healdsburg and downsize. They commissioned
Saitowitz to replace a single-family house with two L-plan houses and
an accessory dwelling unit (ADU) over a shared garage. Each house is
2,600 square feet (241.5 m²) and opens onto a private courtyard through
glass sliders. They are clad in white ribbed-metal panels, with white roofs
to reduce solar gain, and there is an array of solar panels over the ADU.
The development achieves a balance of privacy and sociability and
is a model of how to densify a district of single-family houses without
overwhelming the neighbors.

A three-unit complex that Saitowitz
designed to replace a single-family
house in Healdsburg.

WEAVING THE URBAN FABRIC

Birch House
Los Angeles

GRIFFIN ENRIGHT ARCHITECTS

Midtown Los Angeles was built up in the 1920s as the city expanded westward to either side of Wilshire Boulevard and the tail end of the legendary Route 66, now Santa Monica Boulevard. Block after block of Spanish Colonial bungalows have survived unchanged for a century, but new threads are being woven into this suburban tapestry. The 3,600-square-foot (334.5 m²) Birch House was designed as a radical alternative to its neighbors, which are plopped down in the middle of their lots and make little use of open space or natural light. Here, the architects have turned every corner of the compact 50-by-130-foot (15.2 by 39.6 m) lot to advantage. The two-floor, asymmetrical composition of white cubes with large windows seems to hover over low concrete walls. A glass-enclosed atrium splits it in two, and a ramp descends to a garage half a level below grade.

Steps lead up to a pivoting entry door and the narrow opening morphs into a soaring, light-filled volume beneath a skylight 52-feet long (15.8 m). To either side, on a polished travertine floor, are open living, dining, and kitchen areas, as well as two bedrooms. The gently curved skylight follows the east-west axis of the house, and a polycarbonate shade containing tiny tubes filters the sunlight. Forced perspectives and sensuous curves enrich the spatial adventure, as does the alternation of pale tones with ebonized ceilings and cabinetry. A sculptural staircase of cantilevered wood treads ascends to a glass bridge that spans the atrium, linking the primary suite and the daughter's bedroom. Each has a generous deck from which to gaze over the urban landscape. Pocketing glass sliders open the atrium to a terrace of raw travertine. A sinuous pool lined with indigo mosaic and flanked by a wedge-shaped office-gym and a small garden extends the axis of the skylight into the back yard.

CALIFORNIA HOUSES

The house is the epitome of indoor—outdoor living, with its decks, alfresco seating, and firepits, but its interior employs refined materials and detailing. The open kitchen was designed to have the quality of a living room, with its tigerwood cabinetry and backlit onyx countertop. Rift-cut white oak is employed elsewhere. Seamless expanses of glass are set directly into walls, and their angles create a myriad of reflections. The atrium frames two mature sycamores on the street. A powder room is entirely lined in white pebbles. The owners have made an eclectic selection of contemporary furniture and light fittings to complement the architecture.

Houses as extraordinary as this do not happen by chance. The partnership of Margaret Griffin and John Enright has been pushing the envelope of residential architecture for 25 years. The clients were waiting to make a radical shift from a traditional house. Steven Birch heads an investment advisory firm, and his wife Laura Lemle is an interior designer. They wanted an open plan that would maximize the public areas and connect all the spaces through porous boundaries, and they gave the architects

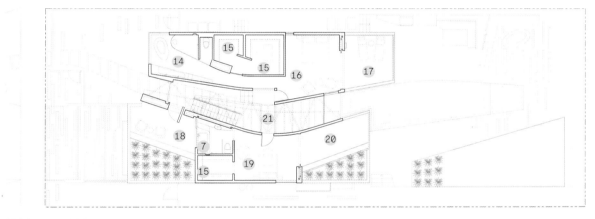

SECOND-FLOOR PLAN

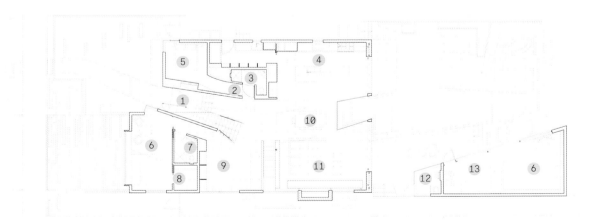

FIRST-FLOOR PLAN

1   Entry hall
2   Powder room
3   Pantry
4   Kitchen
5   Guest bedroom
6   Office
7   Bathroom
8   Closet
9   Family room
10 Dining area
11 Living area
12 Poolside bathroom
13 Exercise room
14 Primary bathroom
15 Closet
16 Primary bedroom
17 Primary deck
18 Front deck
19 Bedroom
20 Bedroom deck
21 Bridge / atrium

WEAVING THE URBAN FABRIC

WEAVING THE URBAN FABRIC

CALIFORNIA HOUSES

a free hand in achieving that goal. Griffin and Enright modeled different versions of the basic concept before refining the design to use a minimum of structural steel. They built out to the sides of the lot and positioned windows high or low to balance the light from the atrium while blocking out neighbors to either side.

Light and space are celebrated in a house that liberates its owners and their fortunate guests to experience the best of southern California living throughout the year. Griffin likens it to a sundial in which there is no need for a clock to judge the time of day. Too many recent additions to the neighborhood are dumb boxes, maxing out their plots. Griffin and Enright have treated their site more imaginatively.

Hollywood Bowl House Venice

DAVID HERTZ ARCHITECTS

David Hertz has been an environmentalist ever since, as a young surfer, he lobbied for the clean-up of Santa Monica Bay, and for most of his practice he lived and worked close to the beach in Venice. Recycling materials and conserving energy are twin passions that inform all his work, and both are showcased in the house he designed for a couple and their children. In a nod to their profession and to the weathered wood cottages of this ocean-front neighborhood, Hertz clad the house and a high fence in century-old cedar boards formerly used as bleachers in the Hollywood Bowl. They are imprinted with seat numbers—a reminder of the multitudes who sat there listening to great music under the stars.

The boards provide a patina and a quiet anonymity to this block-deep, 7,100-square-foot (659.6 m²) house, which shares a double lot with a restored duplex and a vintage clapboard cottage that has been raised and repositioned atop a six-car garage. They conceal its size and ensure privacy for celebrities who prefer this spacious but funky retreat to the glamorous spreads of Malibu and Beverly Hills. One wall hides a covered lap pool, spa, and sauna, another encloses the front yard. At the entry a massive slab of salvaged teak pivots to reveal the central staircase that links the basement to the three floors. To either side, French doors swing wide to open the living and dining rooms to the garden. Boldly shuttered concrete walls (employing boards from the same source for formwork) anchor the house, playing off the soft-toned stucco and recycled oak floors.

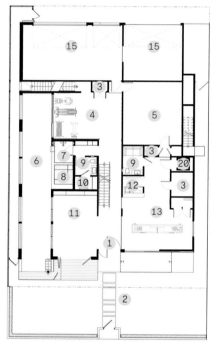

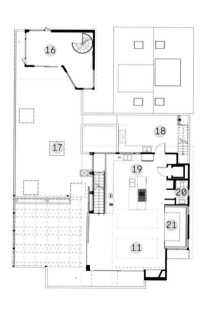

BASEMENT PLAN   FIRST-FLOOR PLAN   SECOND-FLOOR PLAN   THIRD-FLOOR PLAN

1	Entry	9	Powder room	17	Roof deck	25	Living/dining area
2	Front yard	10	Sauna	18	Barbecue area	26	Library
3	Storage	11	Living room	19	Kitchen	27	Courtyard
4	Gym	12	Wet bar	20	Elevator	28	Hall
5	Media room	13	Family room	21	Dining area	29	Laundry
6	Swimming pool	14	Pool equipment	22	Bathroom	30	Walk-in closet
7	Poolside patio	15	Garage	23	Bedroom	31	Roof access
8	Spa	16	Office	24	Child's bedroom		

CALIFORNIA HOUSES

Hertz interwove new and old to create a three-dimensional complex of open spaces, bedrooms, and an office accessed by a spiral stair. The attic of the cottage has been turned into a playroom for small children, and the inner second-floor patio provides a sheltered retreat. The wife's bedroom is intimate and informally furnished, an oasis of stillness and seclusion for a busy actor who may just have returned from a shoot halfway around the world. The window looks out to a narrow gap between two beachfront blocks framing a glimpse of the ocean and a single lanky palm tree. In contrast, there is an open lounge area on the third floor with deep armchairs, a bar, chef's kitchen, and shaded deck. It is an ideal stage for a party, looking out over the eclectic landscape of shingled roofs, lofty palms, and a tangle of overhead wires that the city has not got around to burying.

The interior is bathed in natural light from strategically placed openings and frustum-shaped skylights that pop up from the roof terrace. A clerestory in the wall enclosing the pool admits a bar of westerly sun, which the water reflects into the adjoining gym. A mosaic of small, two-faced photovoltaic panels bonded to clear glass canopies the roof terrace, casting a dappled pattern of light and shade. It generates energy from the light on both sides and supplements a rooftop array of solar panels to cover all energy needs, making the house net-zero.

Thirty miles west, in the hills behind Malibu, Hertz built the Wing House, an even more ambitious demonstration of adaptive re-use. As he began to design a house for a professional woman with a fondness for curvilinear forms, he realized that an airliner offered the ideal combination of strength, lightness, and sleek elegance. He purchased a decommissioned Boeing 747 from a desert graveyard and had it cut into sections and brought to the site by truck and helicopter. Wings and tail stabilizers were installed atop concrete-block walls to create graceful roofs, and there were plans to utilize the nose cone and a section of the fuselage. Lord Foster once named the 747 as his favorite structure for its adaptability, but it is unlikely that even he envisaged so radical a transformation.

The Wing House in the hills above Malibu incorporates pieces of a disassembled Boeing 747.

WEAVING THE URBAN FABRIC

A+M House
Santa Monica

ERIC OWEN MOSS ARCHITECTS

It is unnecessary to ask for a street number: there is no missing the house that Moss designed for himself and his two grown children a block from the Pacific Coast Highway. A sculptural green block, studded with windows, it is taut, enigmatic, and introverted. In its five decades of practice, Eric Owen Moss Architects has never failed to surprise, and this is no exception. However, the 25-person team is best known for the Constructivist exuberance of warehouse conversions adjoining its office in Culver City, an industrial district of Los Angeles that is rapidly becoming a tech hub. This 1,900-square-foot (176.5 m²) house—the firm's first in 20 years—surprises by its reticence.

Moss delights in complexity—of form and thought—though he dismisses the word as overworked. He prefers to describe the house as "the tension between possibilities." Located on a modest 30-by-60-foot (9.1 by 18.3 m) plot, it turns constraints to advantage, squeezing three light-filled floors and a tiny roof deck within the mandatory height limit of 35 feet (10.7 m). A permeable grid of pavers unifies the site, and the house is set back from the street, its neighbors, and a storm drain to the rear. The street front is carved away to either side of the entry to accommodate parking places.

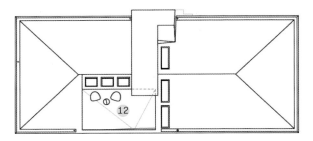

ROOF PLAN

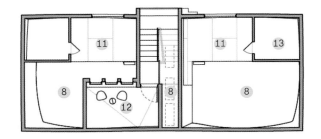

LOFT PLAN

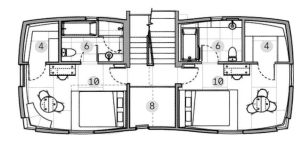

THIRD-FLOOR PLAN

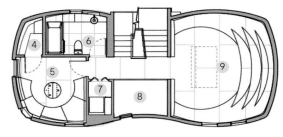

SECOND-FLOOR PLAN

To create a kinetic response to these limitations, Moss and lead architect Eric McNevin laid out the first floor as two 20-foot-diameter (6.1 m) circles and the roof as a rectangle, so that the corners morph from square to round as they descend. Each is subtly different, and the rear wall leans out 5 feet (1.5 m) to add interior space to the upper levels. The irregular fenestration intersects the corners, requiring the glass to be folded in different ways. The wood frame is sprayed with yellowish-green polyurea to create a waterproof skin that McNevin likens to the wet suits worn by surfers. Because this thin protective skin reveals every imperfection in the structure, the frame was constructed as meticulously as a cabinet. Each stud was numbered and CNC-milled to form a kit of parts.

1   Entry
2   Kitchen
3   Dining area
4   Closet
5   Symposium
6   Bathroom
7   Laundry
8   Open
9   Theater
10 Bedroom
11 Loft
12 Deck
13 Mechanical room

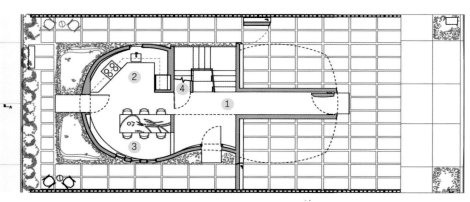

FIRST-FLOOR PLAN

CALIFORNIA HOUSES

WEAVING THE URBAN FABRIC

The house belongs in spirit to Rustic Canyon, a picturesque enclave of Modernism to the east that includes the influential Case Study designs of Richard Neutra and Charles & Ray Eames, alongside a host of contemporary architects. But the immediate surroundings are raffish, with exposed utility poles, chain-link fencing, an expansive parking lot, and a harlequin-patterned block to one side. It is a tribute to the tough self-confidence of Moss that his house is not overwhelmed by this visual chaos.

The front door, as massive as the wall that surrounds it, swings open to an axial hallway with a ceiling of bowed glulam beams, which leads back to a central atrium, a compact kitchen–dining room, and the rear door. Stairs ascend to a subtly curved theater with cushioned bleachers where the family can entertain friends and watch movies on a fold-down screen, or gather in another sitting area to the rear. Bedrooms at front and back occupy the third level, each with a sleeping loft for children. In contrast to the spatial drama of the Lawson-Westen House of 1993, the interior emphasizes calm and comfort. Concrete floors on the first floor give way to birch ply on the staircase and upper floors. The palette is monochromatic.

The absence of drama focuses attention on the details. Almost everything is handcrafted, from the furniture and built-ins to the stair balustrade and other metal elements forged by master metalsmith Tom Farrage. The dining table is a massive sandwich of plywood, incised with a plan of the latest Moss building, topped with acrylic and supported on a steel tube that is squished flat at the base. "It's an aspirational building," says Moss. "It was conceived for my son (a college football player) and daughter (a dancer training at the Julliard School). I wanted them to know that the impossible was possible."

CALIFORNIA HOUSES

See-Through House Santa Monica

KONING EIZENBERG ARCHITECTURE

Serendipity shaped the house that Julie Eizenberg and Hank Koning designed on a residential street a mile from the ocean. A couple who are long-time local residents—she is a climate policy advocate; he runs his family's real-estate management company—gave them the commission. The 32-foot (9.8 m) height limit, complex setbacks, and other zoning regulations are tightly enforced—as the wife well knew, since she and Koning both served on the City Planning Commission. In tracing the maximum allowable envelope, the architects discovered they had the outline of an asymmetrical barn. That delighted the wife, who had grown up in Maine and appreciated the simplicity of the rural vernacular. The side walls and roof of the house are clad in wood shingles; the front and back walls in smooth-troweled white stucco. And the form of the studio that was placed atop the garage at the end of the lot (see pp. 157–59) was inspired by the bonnet worn by a Pennsylvanian Quaker ancestor in an inherited portrait. The studio was wrapped in a white elastomeric membrane, which provides a durable, waterproof seal, requires no maintenance, and links the two buildings visually across the back yard.

Sociability and sustainability are the hallmarks of work by Koning Eizenberg and their team. The 3,100-square-foot (288 m²) residence is aptly named for its openness and use of passive solar strategies. It is set back behind an unfenced front yard, bounded by a low stone wall and a hedge. In contrast to neighboring houses, which turn their backs to the street, the first-floor living area and upstairs primary suite have glass

sliders at front and back. When they are retracted, ocean breezes waft through the house keeping it cool. Sliding screens of cedar-wood slats provide privacy and shade from western sun. Hot air is vented through skylights and angled vents projecting from the row of three children's bedrooms. The owners make little use of the radiant floor heating and air conditioning, and rooftop solar panels lower their energy bills.

The air of simplicity is deceptive: every element of the house has been carefully considered and calibrated. A vine-covered pergola at the front adds a layer of light and shade. Because sliders open up both ends of the house, the sides can be closed so you do not look into neighboring properties. There is an easy flow of space from the sitting area at the front past the dining area to the kitchen, which anchors the zone and becomes the focus of family activity. A pantry adjoins the kitchen; on the other side is a compact office and media room. The custom black-steel and glass sliders have built-in mesh screens to exclude flying insects. A staircase with treads of boldly patterned composite wood runs up one side of the room. The architects have used white pegboard, one of their favorite frugal materials, as a balustrade and to frame deep-set skylights over the book-lined concourse that links the four bedrooms. The clients moved to a larger house to give every family member a separate bedroom but, to encourage sociability, the children share a bathroom. The architects left the owners to select an appealing mix of heritage and classic modern furniture.

WEAVING THE URBAN FABRIC

Koning Eizenberg's experience of navigating the labyrinth of zoning restrictions from both sides of the fence opened loopholes. The height limit would have accommodated a third floor but this was prohibited. However, with a pitched roof you are allowed an attic. The clients needed extra storage, and they can ascend a ladder to access this bonus space. When the room over the garage was built, it was forbidden to include a shower or kitchen because a second dwelling unit was not permitted given the zoning and lot size. Then the rules were changed to encourage the development of backyard ADUs to help address the housing crisis. This one has now become highly desirable, and at night it appears to float over the backlit polystyrene membrane that clads the garage.

1   Entry
2   Living / dining area
3   Pantry
4   Kitchen
5   Office
6   Entertainment room
7   Garage
8   Lounge
9   Laundry
10 Balcony
11 Child's bedroom
12 Primary bedroom
13 Primary closet
14 Primary bathroom
15 Child's bathroom
16 Guest room

FIRST-FLOOR PLAN

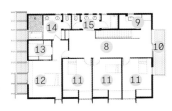

SECOND-FLOOR PLAN

WEAVING THE URBAN FABRIC

Spectral Bridge
Venice

EYRC ARCHITECTS
WITH JOHANNES GIRARDONI

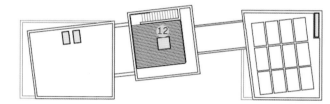

ROOF PLAN

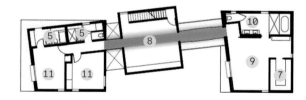

SECOND-FLOOR PLAN

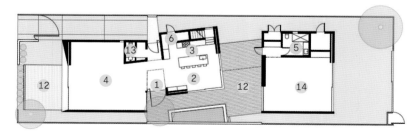

FIRST-FLOOR PLAN

1   Entry
2   Dining area
3   Kitchen
4   Living area
5   Bathroom
6   Pantry
7   Walk-in closet
8   Media lounge
9   Primary bedroom
10 Primary bathroom
11 Guest bedroom
12 Deck
13 Powder room
14 Garage

Architecture, light, and landscape are fused to make the Spectral Bridge, located on a quiet street in Venice, a habitable work of art. Two cubes clad in white stucco flank one in black charred wood. They are linked at the upper level by a glass bridge that glows softly, changing color by day and night. The street façade and the middle block are rotated seven degrees, imparting a sense of motion and animating the spaces to either side. A Corten-steel fence conceals the narrow lot from street and neighbors, giving the owners privacy indoors and out, and the house is entered from the side, through the kitchen in the middle block. The project was conceived by Johannes Girardoni, an Austrian-born artist with a passion for architecture, and realized jointly with EYRC Architects, near neighbors to his studio in Culver City.

Artist and architects found themselves in agreement on the concept of breaking up the mass, rotating the blocks, and creating useful space on three sides, and they worked hand-in-hand on design and construction. As the house was being framed it found an enlightened

WEAVING THE URBAN FABRIC

buyer, a professional couple with two small children. "They understood our ideas, backed our vision, and allowed us to push further than if we had done it for ourselves," says Girardoni.

Materiality is an important feature of the house that Steve Ehrlich, founding partner of EYRC, designed for himself in Venice, and those that he and his partners have realized over the past four decades. "Here we used Shou Sugi Ban (burnt cedar boards) outside and in, a centuries-old Japanese technique for making wood resistant to fire and termites," says Ehrlich. "Synthetic materials have displaced it in Japan, but it's now fabricated by a company in Texas." Its silky texture invites the touch and sunlight reveals the tiny cracks in the sealed charcoal surface. This plays off the steel-troweled stucco, whose whiteness is paradoxically enhanced by the addition of a blue pigment. Polished concrete floors root the house to the land; cabinetry and bedroom floors are natural or stained oak.

There is a Japanese sense of restraint in the architecture and still more in the dry garden, sparingly planted with succulents, a palo verde, and a melaleuca tree. Heidi Girardoni is an artist and therapist, and her skills found expression in the minimalist interiors. She searched for furniture that would match the scale of the living area, selecting sensuous sofas by Zaha Hadid as the dominant element. Pocketing glass sliders open the living–dining area to the front garden, the kitchen to a raised pool, and the rear garage/studio to wood decks.

Stairs ascend from the kitchen to a media room with a projector and a blank wall as screen. Glass-walled bridges connect the children's bedrooms in front and the primary suite to the rear. Sensors are programmed to respond to the shift from dark to light, beginning an hour before sunrise, resuming in the late afternoon, and continuing as late as the owner chooses. They activate the LEDs, which read as continuous

WEAVING THE URBAN FABRIC

strips of light within the resin beams that frame each bridge, slowly changing from white to a variety of hues. Sitting in the spectral lounge you are immersed in a cloud of colored light as though you had strayed into an installation by Dan Flavin. "I wanted to create a site where the boundaries between art and architecture dissolve," Girardoni explains. It's a seamless whole; a living environment in which the light of day and its absence at night, gives way to an illumination in which the participants' experience continuously expands and contracts."

Spectral Bridge is organic and interactive, responding in different ways from one day to another through the year and to the movements of the family. The intensity of the color field changes one's perception of the sky and of other lights in the house, while complementing the monochromatic living areas. To add to the experience, sensors react to the changes of light and generate unearthly sounds corresponding to the frequencies of the colors as they pass from the warm to the cool end of the spectrum.

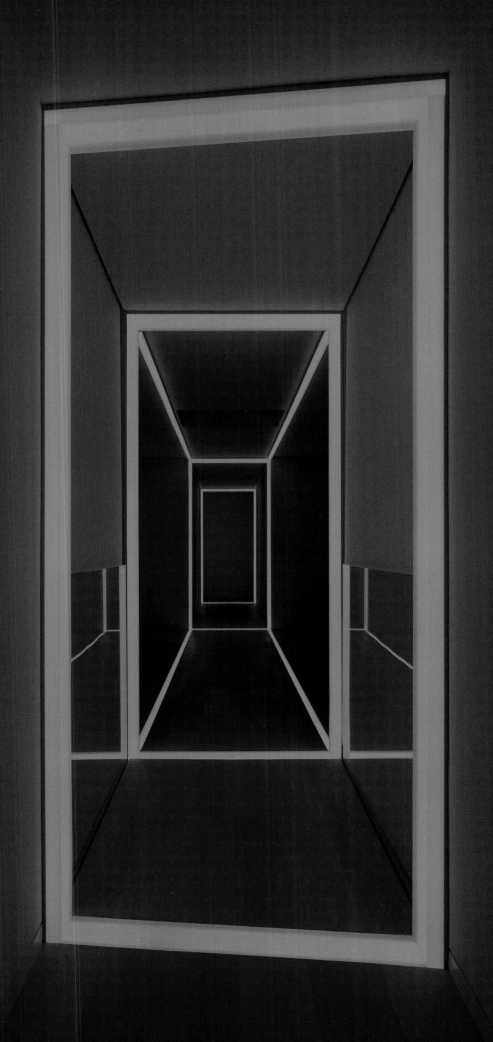

Second House
Culver City

FREELANDBUCK

Culver City grew up during the past century as a blue-collar municipality of modest dwellings, movie studios, and light industry, midway between downtown LA and the ocean. Over the past two decades, low rents lured architects, art galleries, and adventurous restaurants, transforming it into a cultural hub, and the recent influx of big tech companies accelerated the process of gentrification. But the city has retained its gritty character and low-rise density.

A professional couple who owned a lot that was zoned for two houses commissioned David Freeland to design a 1,500-square-foot (139.4 m²) residence for a family member in the confined space immediately behind their existing home. Their requirements were simple: living spaces and two upstairs bedrooms reached from a passage leading back from the street, and a two-car garage accessed from the rear alley. The clients were willing to take a risk on the design and encouraged Freeland, collaborating with his New York partner, Brennan Buck, to explore many different options. The architects have a passion for complex geometries and spatial drama, and they considered 50 variations on a cube, carved away to create a free flow of indoor–outdoor spaces. They wanted to play off the steeply pitched roofs of the old house while creating a holistic composition and staying within the zoning envelope.

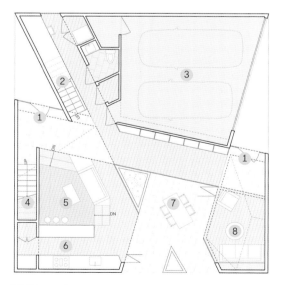

FIRST-FLOOR PLAN

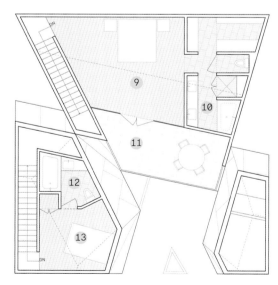

SECOND-FLOOR PLAN

1   Entry
2   Stairs to primary bedroom
3   Garage
4   Stairs to guest bedroom
5   Dining area
6   Kitchen
7   Courtyard
8   Living room
9   Primary bedroom
10 Primary bathroom
11 Deck
12 Guest bathroom
13 Guest bedroom

The choice was narrowed to a few variants and discussed with the clients before they settled on a balance of aggregation and subtraction: three volumes wrapped around a courtyard, and two peripheral wedges of space—one to facilitate access from the alley to the guest parking space, the other to mark the threshold. Walls and roofs have a uniform cladding—a rainscreen of cement panels—which is gray on the orthogonal walls at the outer edges and white on the tilted or angled surfaces that represent cuts in the cube. It is a playful exercise that creates a lively interplay of positive and negative space, light and shadow, making a small house feel much bigger. The wedges of space are echoed in the triangular firepit and planter for succulents that border the courtyard. The rainscreen that wraps the house provides a thermal barrier that moderates extremes of temperature.

WEAVING THE URBAN FABRIC

CALIFORNIA HOUSES

There is a seamless flow of space from the kitchen–dining area through a gallery that serves as a library to the living room, and all three open to the courtyard through folding glass doors. An alternation of gray limestone and white-stained knotty pine in the floors marks the transitions from one zone to another. Two staircases ascend to the bedrooms and one side of each is painted red or orange. Sunlight playing off these surfaces creates a penumbra of color that spills across the white walls, and custom lamps provide vibrant accents in the living areas. Windows in the outer walls are set high for privacy and to focus attention on the sky and a backdrop of mountains rather than the discordant jumble of the immediate surroundings, and the main bedroom has a terrace overlooking the courtyard.

To increase the number of housing options the Los Angeles Planning Department is encouraging the construction of pre-approved ADU designs in the rear yards of single-family houses. Those featured in this book are tiny—a cabin of a few hundred square feet or a room over a garage. Second House might be described as a mega-ADU, occupying found space and providing a rich environment for living. Culver City is setting a lead in loosening zoning restrictions and encouraging the densification of residential areas. FreelandBuck has demonstrated how much that could add in the quantity and quality of housing, and how it could drive down the cost of rent or purchase.

WEAVING THE URBAN FABRIC

Twin House
Santa Monica

KEVIN DALY ARCHITECTS

If the civic authorities of Greater Los Angeles really wanted to resolve the housing crisis, they would stop making pious speeches and empower groups of progressive architects to develop innovative solutions. It would offer a far greater chance of success than relying on a sclerotic bureaucracy. Prototypes would be tested for their livability, affordability, and environmental impact, and the best of them would be built at scale on well-landscaped sites close to public transit hubs. Kevin Daly has shown the way with his exemplary multi-unit complexes, his development of a two-residence lot, and his design of a visionary ADU.

In contrast to the Second House by FreelandBuck (see p. 168), which goes back-to-back with an existing residence, Daly and his team designed a pair of linear, two-floor houses flanking a shear wall that extends from a leafy front yard to double parking places off the rear alley. The goal was to begin a process of densification without changing the character of the neighborhood. The spinal wall blocks sound and jogs to accommodate flights of stairs on either side. Gables are staggered to integrate clerestories that pull in light and cool breezes from both sides and incorporate tiny roof terraces. Side paths link front and back with inset patios at the midway point.

Unlike most developers, Daly chose to enrich the simple geometry of the 2,400-square-foot (223 m²) house his family occupied for two years and the slightly smaller rental unit. The exterior is clad in treated pine boards highlighted by inserts of stainless steel, and the cut-outs with integrally colored stucco. The side entry opens into a double-height living room, lit from above, and this flows into a spacious kitchen and dining area. At the back is a guest bedroom that can double as an office, and there are two bedroom suites and a pair of studies on the second level. The architect designed a screen of red lacquered metal plates to wrap around the stair balustrade. At no point do you feel constrained by the narrow plan, and both houses offer a lively architectural promenade in three dimensions.

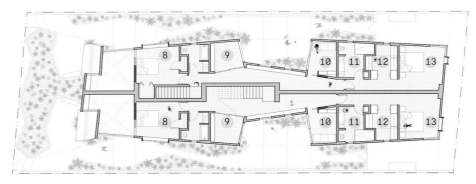

SECOND-FLOOR PLAN

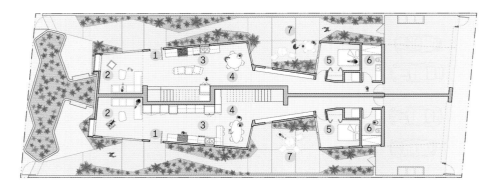

FIRST-FLOOR PLAN

1	Entry
2	Living room
3	Kitchen
4	Dining room
5	Guest bedroom
6	Guest bathroom
7	Courtyard
8	Library
9	Study 1
10	Study 2
11	Primary bathroom
12	Primary closet
13	Primary bedroom

CALIFORNIA HOUSES

WEAVING THE URBAN FABRIC

BI(H)OME PROTOTYPE

Years before LA pre-approved model designs for ADUs, Daly created a prototype as a studio project with his students at UCLA. Named the BI(h)OME, it was designed in the architect's office and erected on campus in a few days. A double membrane of transparent shrink wrap, separated by sections of cardboard tubing to create a thermal barrier, was drawn over a frame of lightweight bent-metal tubing embedded in a plywood platform. Inset plywood frames at either end defined porches that could serve as frames for climbing plants.

The BI(h)OME is a contemporary spin on the yurt: easy to assemble and transport, recyclable and sustainable. A production model could be enlarged to 900 square feet (83.6 m²) and be clad in a tough, translucent membrane of ETFE, a plastic sheeting that is becoming increasingly versatile and durable. Daly would specify a double layer and use a vacuum pump to evacuate the air and create a taut skin. The outer surface would be printed to block glare, ensure privacy, and serve as an integral photovoltaic array. An insulated wood base could contain wiring, plumbing, and radiant heating. Ideally, a manufacturer of ETFE would subsidize design development and sponsor the construction of a hundred units, separated by landscaping like Douglas Burnham's forest cabins in Mendocino (see p. 94). SelgasCano, the acclaimed Spanish firm, created a precedent for such a structure in their 2015 Serpentine pavilion in London, and they recently used a similar lightweight membrane to wrap a house for themselves in the Hollywood Hills.

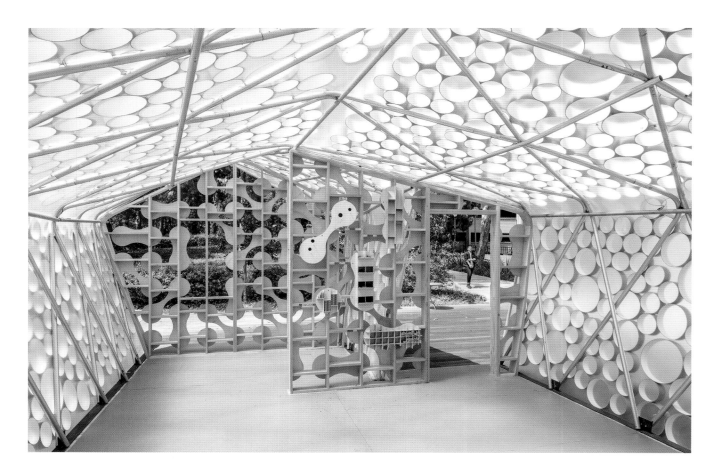

CALIFORNIA HOUSES

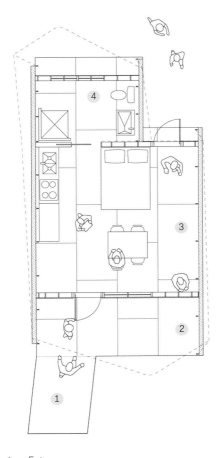

Architects have been experimenting with prefabrication over the past century, but they have never progressed beyond a few pilot projects or achieved economies of scale. The materials were often inappropriate: in the post-war London of my childhood the walls of prefab houses were made from asbestos sheets. By using a minimum of environmentally sensitive materials, a simple lightweight frame, and built-in services and fittings, the dream of home ownership could be made far more affordable. And, when people move, their houses could also be taken down and transported with their other possessions.

1   Entry
2   Porch
3   Bedroom / living space
4   Bathroom / dressing area

WEAVING THE URBAN FABRIC

CALIFORNIA HOUSES

One Half House Sherman Oaks

KATY BARKAN/NOW HERE

A couple with two teenage daughters outgrew their 1946 bungalow in the San Fernando Valley of Los Angeles. They could not afford to buy a larger house so they commissioned Katy Barkan to extend the one they had, adding a second floor, a third bedroom, and nearly doubling the floor area from 1,200 to 2,300 square feet (111.5 to 213.7 m²), on a very tight budget. To complicate Barkan's task, Los Angeles requires that the entire house must meet current energy codes if the addition exceeds 50 per cent. It also had to fit into a tight zoning envelope, so the design went through many iterations before achieving its final form.

"The wife is my sister, so I knew that they were the social center of their block," says Barkan. "Their door is open and they are always ready for a party. They didn't want to appear ostentatious or grand, so I had to find middle ground between standing out and fitting in." The clients gave her a free hand and she came up with a brilliant solution that plays inventive variations on the suburban aesthetic of stucco walls and shingled gables. Half the bungalow was stripped to its studs, rebuilt to meet current standards, and painted dark gray. The light-gray addition that replaces the other half is set back a few feet in deference to the single-floor houses to either side. The playful geometry of a folded roof and a diagonal shadow line break up the mass.

The new wing is pivoted to maintain the minimum set back between the corner of the house and the rear garage. That introduces a narrow, skylit wedge of space between new and old, linking the two levels and drawing guests through the house. Oak floorboards run parallel to the perimeter of the house, marking the diverging axes. The primary bedroom is tucked inside the entry, but the rest of the first floor is free-flowing, with glass sliders opening the living room to a back yard set up for entertaining. The upper floor is the daughters' domain. Though the house is flooded with light from above and from the expansive glazing to the rear it remains cool through the torrid summers of the San Fernando Valley. Projecting eaves shade the glass and light-toned asphalt shingles reduce solar gain. Recessed gutters channel water into a storage tank from which it can be drawn to irrigate the drought-resistant plantings of landscape designer Robert Pressman.

1   Entry
2   Office
3   Dining area
4   Primary bedroom
5   Primary bathroom
6   Kitchen
7   Powder room
8   Living room
9   Outdoor dining area
10   Deck
11   Pool house
12   Pool
13   Kid's hangout
14   Laundry room
15   Kid's bathroom
16   Bedroom

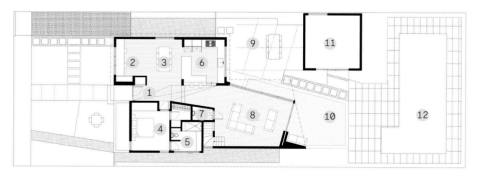

FIRST-FLOOR PLAN

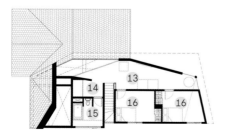

SECOND-FLOOR PLAN

CALIFORNIA HOUSES

CALIFORNIA HOUSES

The post-war suburbs that replaced the citrus orchards of the Valley (remember the movie *Chinatown*) have a deadening monotony. They are the province of tract home builders, lacking any architectural character, and that makes Barkan's intervention all-the-more significant. It is deceptively simple in its form and materiality, yet enigmatic and compelling. It is distinctive but feels right at home: a modest, low-cost solution to a family's needs that enriches their lives and the experience of their neighbors, outside and in. It should inspire other residents to make more of what they have and raise the bar on design. It is also a notable achievement for a small, fledgling practice. Barkan pursued a career in architecture by chance after studying comparative literature and working at *Artforum* magazine. But she was mentored by Preston Scott Cohen at Harvard Graduate School of Design and worked for two leading East Coast firms before opening her LA office and winning the Rome Prize. Few practitioners have laid such a solid foundation.

VIEWING TOWN & COUNTRY

In the James Ivory adaptation of E. M. Forster's classic novel, *A Room with a View* (1908), a young couple thrill to a tightly framed glimpse of Florence cathedral from the window of their pension, and that prospect is hard to top. In California, where open spaces far outnumber storied landmarks, owners seek panoramic vistas encompassing buildings and nature. The hazy expanse of the Los Angeles basin becomes a glittering sea of lights after dark, and the view from the Hollywood Hills can be as impressive as the spectacle from a descending plane.

In the 1930s, inaccessible and unstable sites in those hills were given away as premiums for subscribers to *Sunset* magazine. Almost anyone could afford to build there, often without a permit, perching on a slope or propping a lightweight shelter on poles. Now, a thicket of city and state hillside regulations mandate caissons and retaining walls, while limiting height and ground coverage. These constraints spur architects to be inventive, just as the steep slopes brought out the best in Schindler, Harris, Ain, and other pioneer Modernists.

There are few empty lots remaining in LA, and mega-mansions are displacing modest bungalows in the hills as on the flats. Occasionally, great size and originality come together. Elsewhere, from Palm Springs, north to Ojai, Napa, and Mendocino counties, owners can gaze out to mountains, canyons, and forests. Architects are at pains to conceal or break up the mass of such additions to avoid overwhelming the natural surroundings. A house with a commanding view has a responsibility to preserve the beauty of its own situation.

Collywood
West Hollywood

OLSON KUNDIG

CALIFORNIA HOUSES

SECOND-FLOOR PLAN

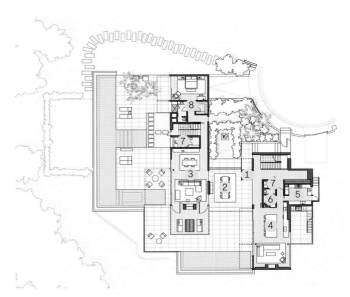

FIRST-FLOOR PLAN

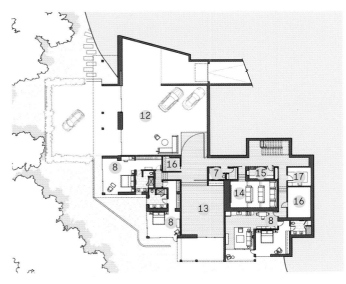

LOWER-FLOOR PLAN

This house could be described as a kinetic sculpture: Donald Judd meets Alexander Calder. The structural steel frame and precise details have affinities with the former, while the airy, playful character of doors and windows evoke the latter, as do the red steel plates that define the street entry. The client, a financier who has lived around the world, is an adventurous spirit who loves to entertain and shares with his architect a passion for the outdoors. During his years as a movie producer, he bought a spur of the Hollywood Hills above Sunset Boulevard and commissioned a residence that would be a stage for hospitality and a retreat for himself.

"The owner had few requests but wanted to conduct a conversation, making him an ideal client," recalls Tom Kundig. "For me, houses are all about prospects and refuge. Here the challenge was to grab the big landscape while providing a feeling of intimacy in a succession of rooms that flow into each other and allow friends and business colleagues to congregate. The views extend from the San Gabriel Mountains to the east to the Channel Islands in the west. But, as I explained to him, that's like listening to Wagner for five hours; you should pull back and enjoy the limited views from within the house." Two unsightly mansions, above and below the site, are screened out, but the office and living area look back to the hillside.

1 Entry
2 Dining room
3 Living room
4 Kitchen
5 Dirty kitchen
6 Pantry
7 Powder room
8 Guest suite
9 Primary suite
10 Primary closet
11 Gym
12 Garage
13 Game room
14 Theater
15 Wine storage
16 Storage
17 Laundry

From the street, it would be hard to guess that the house has 15,600 square feet (1,449.3 m²) of enclosed space on three levels. The two upper levels are concealed by concrete walls and steel plates, and the third is buried. Behind this impassive L-plan façade, the house extends out to 7,000 square feet (650.3 m²) of decks on different levels, bracketed by pools on three sides. These terraces are ideal for large fundraisers, while the fireplaces and radiant panels make sitting outside agreeable, even on chilly evenings. The south front is expressed as two separate volumes complemented by a slatted canopy to the west and a wing cantilevered 16 feet (4.9 m) out to the east. The pools act as reflectors bouncing light indoors and demarcating the main terrace. Window walls rise and descend like guillotines, retract or pivot to blur the boundary between open and enclosed, drawing breezes through the house.

Staircases are treated as sculptures, their treads and rails forming a geometrical pattern against a board-marked concrete wall that is raked with sunlight. An expansive primary suite, gym, office, and a series of roof decks occupy the upper floor. The lower level serves the owner's interests, with a garage–gallery for his car collection, a game room and home theater, plus a viewing platform cantilevered off the hillside. Cedar ceilings and oak floors complement the steel and concrete. A powder room borrows from the Japanese tradition of Shou Sugi Ban, scorching timber to improve its resistance to fire. Here it has been used to decorative effect, by wire-brushing cypress wood and giving it a light toast.

Kundig and his team incorporated some of the ingenious mechanisms that are a recurring feature of his work. In an age of smart houses and digital devices, there is something deeply satisfying in his homage to the machine. Pulleys are counterbalanced so that shutters and the heavy garage door can be raised by hand, tubular-metal light pendants may be pulled up and down, and the dining table rolled onto the terrace. Though Kundig does not choose to design every detail in the tradition of Mies, Alvar Aalto, and Jacobsen, he seeks consistency. That prompted him to custom design furniture and devices he cannot find in a catalogue, then put them into limited production. "It pains me when an owner messes up an interior," says Kundig. "You spend so long getting everything right and then someone brings in a La-Z-Boy recliner."

VIEWING TOWN & COUNTRY

JArzm House
Silver Lake

JOHN FRIEDMAN ALICE KIMM
ARCHITECTS (JFAK)

From its title (the initials of each family member's first name) to its transparent, interconnected volumes, this house is a paragon of domesticity. A hybrid of organic and orthogonal forms, stacked and layered on a steep, downhill site, it is a fun place to live and full of surprises. The two partners collaborate closely in their work, but take the lead in turn on most jobs. Here, Alice Kimm played client and gave her husband a free hand on the design. "We had been living on the other side of the hill and bought this empty lot in 2002," recalls John Friedman. "After a long wait—there was always something else to do—I was nudged by my 13-year-old daughter who wondered if she'd ever get to live there."

He placed the house below the street to enclose 3,700 square feet (343.7 m²) on three levels—more than would have been allowed had he lined the house up with its neighbors. As a bonus, the side windows frame dense greenery. Stairs wind down to a tiny entry court, an open living-dining-kitchen area wrapped around a service core, and two kids' bedrooms concealed behind a hinged bookcase. A staircase descends to the parents' suite, their small, stepped offices, and a third bedroom, then down again to a family room that opens onto a pool terrace.

This looks across to the steel canopy that shades the roof of a 540-square-foot (50.2 m²) ADU over the garage at the bottom of the slope. It can serve as a guest house, accessed from above or from a lower street; the upper level is wrapped in shocking pink stucco and has a picture window. Though highly original, the complex fits comfortably into the picturesque, leafy ensemble of small houses that fill the slopes surrounding the Silver Lake Reservoir. Richard Neutra built his VDL Research House on the far shore in 1933, and this bohemian community has been fertile ground for Modernists ever since.

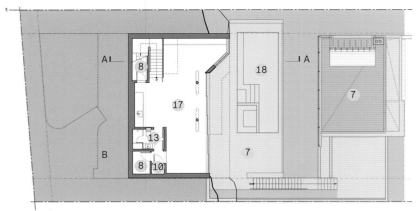

THIRD-FLOOR PLAN

1   Entry
2   Dining area
3   Kitchen
4   Bedroom
5   Bathroom
6   Living area
7   Terrace
8   Closet
9   Crane
10 Mechanical room
11 Laundry
12 Primary bedroom
13 Primary bathroom
14 Office
15 Primary shower
16 Primary bathtub
17 Family room
18 Pool
19 Rentable studio apartment
20 Garage
21 Staircase

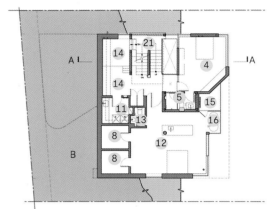

SECOND-FLOOR PLAN

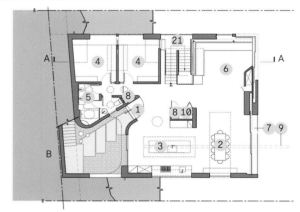

FIRST-FLOOR PLAN

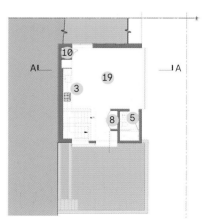

STUDIO APARTMENT PLAN

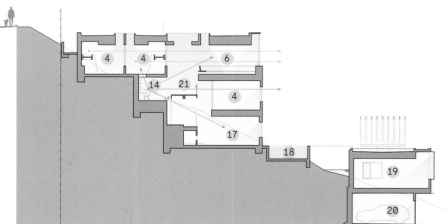

SECTION AA

CALIFORNIA HOUSES

What sets JArzm apart from its progenitors is its openness and the
inventiveness of detail. The flat roof is a fifth façade where a panoply
of skylights alternates with solar panels. The forecourt is treated as a
dry zen garden, embraced by its curved white walls and dominated by a
statuesque *Euphorbia royleana*. It reveals the interior, lit from three sides
and above, with sliders that retract to make indoor dining feel alfresco and
draw in breezes that temper the heat of summer. The trees to either
side provide shade, while defining a panorama of the natural bowl
and the lake. Friedman pays tribute to Alvaro Siza, one of his mentors
at Harvard, in the purity of the all-white composition, but he has brought
his own twist. "We like the dialogue between the different languages,"
he says, "the way the curve descends and reveals itself in fragments."

Friedman called on Chris Berkson, a talented craftsman he has used many times, to fabricate his inventions. A sliding crane runs along the ceiling of the dining area to convey dishes from the kitchen to the terrace two floors down, or even to transport the lightweight aluminum dining table with its retractable legs to poolside. Behind the custom banquette in the living area a rotating steel armature raises and lowers upholstered headrests, which double as a safety barrier to save children bouncing on the cushions from tumbling into the stairwell. The handrail—often an afterthought for architects—is a precisely composed work of art that plays off the glass guardrail. A three-floor screen wall composed of nine different white aluminum units, prefabricated and bolted together, holds books and objects. All that is missing is a second crane to access the highest shelves.

For the children, it was worth the wait. In two of their bedrooms bunk beds are bathed in LED lights and reached by ladders; the third is linked to the stairs by a glass bridge. Even the cats are well served, with little openings that allow them to roam freely. First occupied during the Covid pandemic, the house became a live—work refuge for the entire family.

VIEWING TOWN & COUNTRY

VIEWING TOWN & COUNTRY

CALIFORNIA HOUSES

VIEWING TOWN & COUNTRY

Skyhouse
Beverly Hills

XTEN ARCHITECTURE

The Bird streets, each named for a different avian species, offer expansive views from the Hollywood Hills in a community that is filling up with large contemporary houses. A young professional couple with a teenage son bought a property at the end of a cul-de-sac overlooking a canyon. They then invited XTEN to replace a conventional 1950s residence that made little use of the site. "At our first meeting we noticed a Richard Neutra drawing on their wall, so we knew that they had a serious interest in modern architecture," recalls co-principal Monika Haefelfinger and her partner, Scott Utterstrom. "They wanted a clean-lined, light-filled house and the husband expressed an interest in the landscaping, but she told us, 'This is your baby—we trust you'."

Their faith was vindicated, for the 9,500-square-foot (882.6 m²), L-plan house is an oasis of serenity, facing out to the green wall of the canyon and a glimpse of the ocean, but entirely secluded from its neighbors. Only the roof planes of those higher up the hillside are visible from the terrace. The architects had to stay within the 14-foot (4.3 m) height limit that applies to all the houses in this community, and they turned that constraint to advantage by giving every upper-level room a lofty ceiling.

Two white walls and a bead-blasted stainless-steel gate set up on a grassy rise conceal the house from the street, and a ramp leads down to an expansive garage. Behind the gate is a tiny courtyard with a reflecting pool lined in black terrazzo, and a pivoting glass door. A retractable steel grid shields a dry garden.

Within, circulation space flows around four enclosed areas: an office and a pair of bedrooms that look out to the courtyard; and the living area and primary bedroom that open onto the terrace. Internal vistas complement distant views. An open staircase with a recessed handrail leads down to a basement that burrows into the hillside and contains a game area and screening room in addition to the garage. A gym looks out onto a narrow ledge of plantings that drops away precipitously beyond the glass balustrade.

Collaboration is the rule at XTEN, but the Swiss experience of Haefelfinger and the German heritage of project architect Anina Bach is evident in the minimalist aesthetic, the black and white palette, and the precision of every joint and detail. "Monika and I are involved from start to finish," says Utterstrom. "There isn't a hand-off moment; design decisions happen in team review."

The circulation areas are softly lit from truncated skylights with filtered glass, and the black grid enclosing these coffers complements the slender black steel frames of the windows and pocketing sliders. The custom Bulthaup kitchen with its black cabinetry plays off the white terrazzo floor and the walls of white plaster and tumbled travertine.

1   Entry
2   Office
3   Kitchen
4   Living area
5   Primary bedroom
6   Primary bathroom
7   Bedroom
8   Outdoor courtyard
9   Guest bedroom
10   Gym
11   Media room
12   Bar
13   Garage
14   Rainwater cisterns

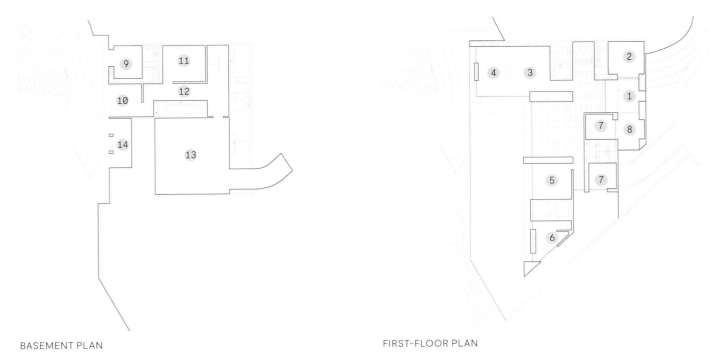

BASEMENT PLAN

FIRST-FLOOR PLAN

VIEWING TOWN & COUNTRY

Mesh blinds serve as a screen for the shadows cast by trees, infusing a rigorous exercise in abstract geometry with the organic shapes of nature. The architects were as concerned with sustainability as aesthetics. The building pad was extended, but the balance of cut and fill was calculated to minimize the amount of excavation. Skylights reduce the need for artificial lighting and rainwater is collected in a cistern and used to irrigate the landscaping. The basement employs the thermal mass of the earth for natural cooling.

This description and the photographs may suggest an interior of chilly perfection, unwelcoming to everyday life. In fact, the couple delighted in the purity of line and surface. When they moved, a new owner, who had previously lived in a Richard Meier house, was equally enthusiastic. The circulation areas now function as a gallery for an eclectic collection of contemporary art.

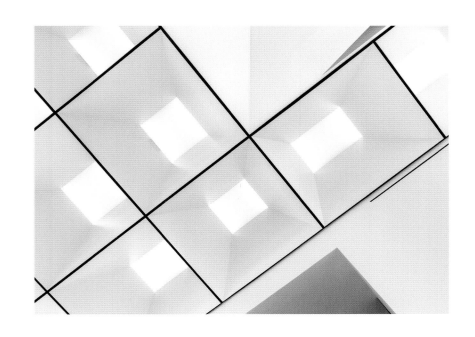

VIEWING TOWN & COUNTRY

CALIFORNIA HOUSES

VIEWING TOWN & COUNTRY

Casa per Amici Santa Monica

MICHAEL KOVAC DESIGN STUDIO

Los Angeles is full of mundane houses that occupy extraordinary sites but fail to exploit their potential. They face away from views and have little space for outdoor living. Many were thrown up during the post-war boom when undeveloped land was still abundant and cheap, construction costs were low, and newly married arrivals were in a hurry to put a roof over their heads. Art and Pat Antin, a couple who moved from New York to southern California, bought such a house on the side of Santa Monica Canyon and lived there for 20 years while raising a family. They met Michael Kovac through a mutual interest in the great outdoors, became friends on a cycling trip to Europe, and invited him to freshen up their house. "I explained to them that they could spend a lot of money on improvements, and it would still be deficient," recalls Kovac. "Finally, they agreed to start from scratch."

The new house was limited to two floors above ground to stay within the 32-foot (9.8 m) height limit, so the hillside was excavated to accommodate a basement. Initially, the program was quite modest: living areas at entry level, a primary suite upstairs, three small guest bedrooms, and recreational facilities downstairs. But, as they discussed the design, the owners' wish list grew to include a screening room, golf simulator, billiards room, wine store, and cushioned bleachers with a pull-down screen in the basement; a pool on the living-room terrace; and twin offices, bathrooms, and walk-in closets on the upper level. The size increased to 6,900 square feet (641 m²).

That challenged Kovac's team to break up the mass of the house so that it would not overwhelm its neighbors and to satisfy the wife's desire that it be warm and friendly. The house is set well back from the street, with a wooden walkway winding through a landscaped front yard beside the garage. A softly curved bay and boundary wall of smooth white plaster complement a chamfered bay clad in thermally treated ash boards. From the entry you look through pocketing glass sliders that open the living areas to the terrace and a panoramic view over the canyon and out to the ocean. A motorized glass rail can be recessed into the ground.

Kovac is renowned for his refined use of materials, and here he had an opportunity to display his creativity to the full. Rift-cut oak cabinetry enhances the hand-troweled plaster walls, as well as the white oak floor and ceiling panels. During construction, the steel structural frame reminded the husband of industrial lofts in New York, and he urged the architect to leave it exposed. Kovac thought that full exposure would be messy, but he carved out three rounded openings in the plywood, exposing steel members and wood joists while incorporating down lighting over the leather-textured quartzite kitchen counter, the dining table, and the sitting area. The spiral staircase linking the three levels is balustraded in a ribbon of blackened steel.

1   Entry
2   Office
3   Closet
4   Bathroom
5   Terrace
6   Primary bedroom
7   Dining area
8   Kitchen
9   Pantry
10   Elevator
11   Powder room
12   Garage
13   Barbecue deck
14   Living area
15   Den
16   Pool deck
17   Spa
18   Pool
19   Game room
20   Golf simulator
21   Theater
22   Bedroom
23   Laundry
24   Wine cellar
25   Outdoor covered courtyard

BASEMENT PLAN

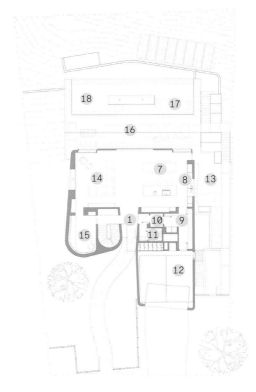

FIRST-FLOOR PLAN

SECOND-FLOOR PLAN

VIEWING TOWN & COUNTRY

CALIFORNIA HOUSES

Casa per Amici lives up to its name. It is tactile and full of natural light. There is an oculus over the jacuzzi opening off the husband's bathroom, and a butterfly roof incorporates clerestories over the main bedroom. A lap pool bridges the lower-level terrace, and a slot window of triple-laminated glass at its base pulls light into the subterranean spaces. Wind off the ocean provides natural cooling, while sustainable features and battery back-up systems are fully integrated within the structure. The house works equally well as a belvedere for gazing out and as an elegant and restrained oasis of calm, enriched by well-matched tones and textures.

Fisher House Ojai

FREDERICK FISHER AND PARTNERS

The 4,000-square-foot (370 m²) house that Frederick Fisher built for his family in Ojai—a bucolic town 80 miles (130 km) northwest of downtown Los Angeles—is an expression of his quiet artistry: a modern interpretation of a Tuscan hilltop villa imbued with the earthy spirit of farm buildings. A three-level cube of prefabricated structural panels, well insulated against the heat of summer, is linked to a single-level wing that opens onto a loggia and provides separate accommodations for two sons. Post Covid, it has become the architect's preferred workplace.

Inspiration came from the six months Fisher spent in residence at the American Academy in Rome, exploring the Italian countryside and sketching as he traveled. The topography and light of Ojai resembles that of Tuscany, and the Fisher house responds to the site: a nine-acre former olive farm that commands sweeping views over the valley to the Topatopa Mountains. It is oriented to the east where expansive windows pull in the morning sun and the glow of sunset is reflected off the peaks. Openings to the south are small and a eucalyptus shades the one large window on the western side. Double glazing affords good insulation and UV protection for artworks without recourse to shades.

An outer skin of corrugated Corten steel adds protection from wildfires and requires no maintenance. The material also reminds the couple of their roots; Jennie Prebor, an art-world veteran, grew up in Pittsburg, and Fisher was raised in Ohio among rusted farm buildings and the decaying industrial plants of Cleveland. Corten steel has a soft texture and weathers like an organic material, with sunlight revealing tones of red, purple, and orange that tie it into the rocky landscape. Steps lead down the slope to the olive grove, a new lap pool, and a shingled 1920s guest cottage where the couple lived during construction.

VIEWING TOWN & COUNTRY

FIRST-FLOOR PLAN

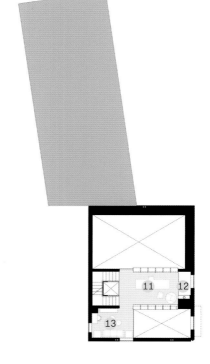

MEZZANINE-FLOOR PLAN

SECOND-FLOOR PLAN

Sybaritic, light-infused volumes are contained within the rigorous shell. The double-height living–dining area is divided from the equally lofty kitchen by a free-standing cabinet and a mezzanine library. Steps ascend to the parents' bedroom suite and the wife's study on the top floor. "A basket of books" is the architect's term for the library. Open wood shelves rise floor to ceiling and are backed with chicken wire so that, from below, the books seem to float in mid-air.

This bridge heightens the impact of the double-height spaces to either side. A chandelier of cylinders suspended from a metal hoop lights the living area with its purple sofas and Art Deco Chinese rug. A vintage American flag that graced the wedding of Fred's great-, great-grandparents presides over this room, along with Nolli's classic map of Rome. Throughout the house, there is an eclectic mix of modern and vintage artworks and furniture. Roy McMakin was commissioned to design the kitchen after the owners had determined the placement of ranges, sinks, and a breakfast table that is lapped by morning sun. The functional layout is enriched with bold colors—a scarlet lacquered island and a pair of vibrant yellow stools—and the witty details that are this designer's hallmark.

1   Entry hall
2   Mud room
3   Powder room
4   Loggia
5   Bedroom
6   Bathroom
7   Family room
8   Utility room
9   Living / dining area
10 Kitchen
11 Library
12 Built-in daybed
13 Study
14 Primary bedroom
15 Wardrobe
16 Deck
17 Built-in bench

An asymmetrical metal trellis functions as a stair balustrade and a frame for the bedroom terrace. A math professor wrote a one-line program, and software generated a birds'-nest pattern. For the house, Fisher's computer-savvy associates tweaked the program to produce a pattern that would meet building codes and could be laser-cut from steel. It serves as a sculptural ribbon that ties the different levels together, casts intricate shadows onto the black-stained wooden stair treads, and is silhouetted against the sky at one corner of the house as though the steel cladding were fraying.

Fisher describes his approach to the house as "long life, loose fit." Every room frames a different vista, and trees block neighboring houses from view. The interior stays cool on the hottest days of summer and ceiling fans limit the need for air conditioning. The steel box opens up to terraces and the shady loggia for year-round outdoor living. From their bed, the owners can watch the sun rise in the morning and the moon follow a similar course at night, so that the rhythms of nature are deeply embedded in their home.

CALIFORNIA HOUSES

VIEWING TOWN & COUNTRY

Desert Canopy House
Palm Springs

SANDER ARCHITECTS

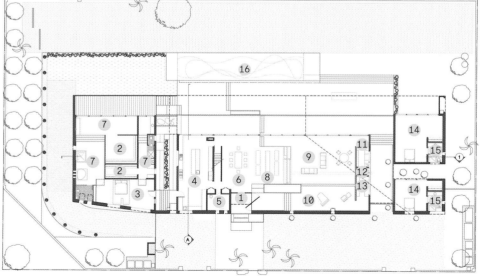

1   Main entry
2   Primary closet
3   Primary bedroom
4   Kitchen
5   Powder room
6   Dining area
7   Primary bathroom
8   Living area
9   Family room
10 Gallery
11 Bar
12 Powder room
13 Storage
14 Guest bedroom
15 Guest bathroom
16 Swimming pool

CALIFORNIA HOUSES

Summer temperatures in Palm Springs can exceed 120 degrees Fahrenheit (49 degrees Celsius), and a couple living there in a Mission-style house were paying $3,000 a month for air conditioning as far back as 2010. That inspired them to commission a new home from Whitney Sander, an architect who achieves a high level of sustainability and economy by using a hybrid building system. His great uncle co-founded the Butler Manufacturing Company in Kansas City, Missouri, in 1901, producing grain storage bins and then branching out into prefabricated industrial buildings and even airplanes.

Charles & Ray Eames's steel-framed Case Study House used off-the-shelf elements for the frame and infill. Such structures never achieved wide popularity and, as the price of steel has soared, all but the largest California houses continue to be framed in wood. The Butler system is affordable, but few consider using it for residential buildings. Sander employed that system to house a friend in Culver City at minimal cost, customizing the infill of a steel frame that was shipped to the site in pieces and rapidly assembled. The success of that project inspired him to explore other ways of using factory-made frames.

The clients wanted the house to face west toward the spectacular backdrop of the San Jacinto Mountains. To protect it from the sun, Sander took his cues from the armadillo and the cactus, both of which have several layers of insulation, and split the house into four pods: a living room sandwiched between the owners' suite to the south and two guest suites to the north. These are separated by 10-feet-wide (3 m) breezeways and shaded by a canopy that projects 17 feet (5.2 m) beyond the west façade to block the summer sun. In winter, the low sun penetrates the glass and helps warm the concrete floors. The breezeways create intimate spaces around each pod, enhancing a sense of privacy, and a hot tub is tucked into one of them.

A local workshop fabricated the exposed metal frame, which imparts a rhythm to the living area and supports a first layer of insulation. This is topped with structurally integrated panels (SIPs) containing rigid foam and sealed with a micro-thin double-reflective building wrap. A rooftop array of solar panels provides all the energy, making this the first net-zero house in Palm Springs.

American contractors, coast to coast, are building houses in the same messy, time-consuming way they were a century ago. A hybrid system of this kind is fast, clean, and avoids waste. It takes full advantage of off-site prefabrication without being constrained by its functionality. In fact, you would never guess that the bone structure of this house shares its DNA with a storage shed. Sculpted concrete panels, inspired by the diamond patterns that waves etch into the sands of Venice beach, clad the house on three sides.

An extended living room accounts for most of the 6,200-square-feet (576 m²) of enclosed space, and it is stepped down to give greater height to the principal gathering area and to demarcate it from the dining area, cushioned media room, and kitchen. On a flat lot, this introduces a pleasing variety. Steel and concrete are impeccably detailed, giving the interior the beauty of minimalist sculpture on display at DIA Beacon; industrial materials transformed into a work of art. The monochromatic palette is enlivened with splashes of color from paintings and the red dining chairs.

To the west, the form of the house is subtly angled, and its mass is reduced by the separation of elements and by floating the south end off the ground. The canopy wraps around to frame the house at either end, arching up to form a terrace outside the owners' bedroom. A lawn, irrigated by gray water, evokes a desert oasis flanked by the ubiquitous palms, and plantings block any glimpse of the neighbors. The mountains appear as borrowed landscape, glowing in the morning sun and turning into black silhouettes in the late afternoon. Here, one can re-create the magical sense of remoteness that drew early settlers.

High Horse Ranch
Mendocino County

KIERANTIMBERLAKE

KieranTimberlake may be best known for the fortress-like US Embassy in London and its additions to US universities, but it has also designed several prefabricated houses, which spurred a commission to build a second home on a site of great natural beauty 140 miles (225 km) north of San Francisco. The clients live in a renovated warehouse in the gritty Mission District and purchased a 64-acre site that was formerly a clandestine marijuana farm with a monastery in the valley below: sin and saintliness side by side. Meadows alternate with steep slopes forested with oaks, madrone, Douglas fir, and ponderosa pine.

To capture the drama of the site, the architects located the house on a ridge, finding a clear patch where only one small tree had to be removed. It is accessed from a winding drive and enjoys vistas of a canyon to the north from the main bedroom and the valley to the south from the living room. One guest cabin is located 100 feet (30.5 m) above the main residence, another is 50 feet (15.2 m) below, and each floats free of the ground on concrete posts. To speed construction in this remote location all three structures were composed of wood modules, fabricated in a factory in San José, trucked to an assembly area, and craned onto the foundations in a day and a half.

VIEWING TOWN & COUNTRY

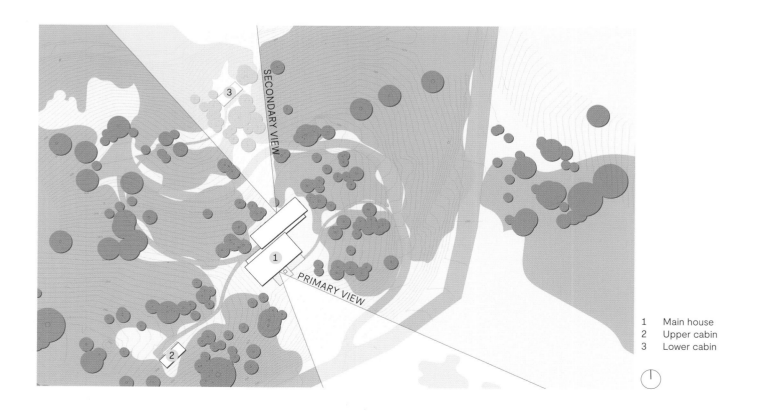

1 Main house
2 Upper cabin
3 Lower cabin

CALIFORNIA HOUSES

VIEWING TOWN & COUNTRY

The 2,580-square-foot (239.7 m²) house comprises a living pavilion and a sleeping pavilion that slip past each other to either side of a thick wall containing mechanical services and a wet zone. Fifteen modules up to 25-feet (7.6 m) long were linked with steel flitch plates to create a seismically resilient shell that was fitted out on site. Full-height glass doors pivot open on one side of the living room and the end of the main bedroom, and are shaded by the cantilevered roof deck that juts 12 feet (3.7 m) out to the south. The roof deck offers shade in summer while allowing the sun to penetrate in winter. Thermals ascend from below and clerestories can be opened to provide cross ventilation. A pierced Corten-steel rainscreen that breathes and weathers to a tone resembling tree bark shields from fire. There are misters on the terrace and the fire service can pump water from a 10,000-gallon storage tank and a pond below. Photovoltaic panels and a generator cover the modest power requirements, a white roof membrane reduces solar gain, and the house is off the grid.

The simplicity of the form is a foil to the spectacle of nature. The ceilings are lined with hard pine and redwood to link the interior with the indigenous trees, the floors are granite, and white lacquered composite panels enclose the service areas. A vibrant geometrical mural by a friend of the owners enlivens the living room, and a shared study adjoins the primary bedroom. The cabins are miniatures of the house, employing the same materials. Their terraces are turned away from the house to assure privacy for any guest who cares to sunbathe in the nude with only wildlife for company.

The owners are a couple with two grown sons, and they were closely involved in the design as the architects considered the best placement and orientation of the house, staking out the footprint to maximize the views and conceal the public road below. They installed weather-recording devices on the ridge prior to construction, supplying the architects with a year's worth of data. "That gave us an understanding of the micro-climate and helped shape the design," says James Timberlake. The approach was carefully planned to isolate the parking area and the turn-around for fire trucks, with paths leading to the three residential structures and an old barn that now serves as a photography studio. Everywhere there is a sense of discovery: as you emerge from the woods, enter the house, and look back.

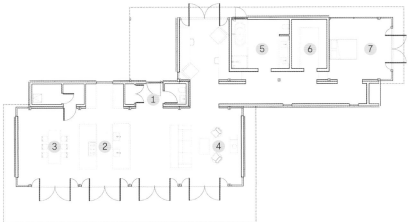

MAIN-HOUSE PLAN

1 Entry
2 Kitchen
3 Dining area
4 Living area
5 Bathroom
6 Closet
7 Bedroom

CALIFORNIA HOUSES

Mount Veeder Outpost Napa County

ATELIER JORGENSEN

Minimalist architects and designers believe in subtraction as the path to perfection and feel they have achieved an ideal form when there is nothing left to take away. That concept inspired Brandon Jorgensen when he was commissioned to design a new house to replace one that had been destroyed in a wildfire. So great was the heat that the concrete pad had been shattered, and two vehicles had been reduced to a puddle of molten metal. The owners, Ridgie and Buttons Barton, own a film-production company in southern California, and they used to drive north to vacation on this hillside overlooking Napa Valley. Rather than mourn the loss of their old house, they saw its destruction as fortuitous. It had been built on spec from a kit and was badly oriented, with the living room looking onto the parking area and guest bedrooms hogging the view. Now they had the opportunity to acquire a house tailored to their tastes in which to live full time and welcome their two grown daughters who live close by.

Although they own over three acres, 1,300-feet (396.2 m) up on the side of Mount Veeder, county regulations required that the new house occupy the same footprint as the old and be only 25 per cent larger. Jorgensen turned these constraints to advantage. He made a succession of 40 models, starting with an asymmetrical cube and carving it away until he had achieved a distinctive form that contained the allowable 2,300 square feet (213.7 m²) of enclosed space.

VIEWING TOWN & COUNTRY

A winding drive ascends to the garage and steps lead up to a flat gravel pad from which the ground drops steeply away. The entry façade comprises three canted planes of corrugated metal in a deep umber tone that picks up on the fire-scarred redwoods flanking the house. The joints are highlighted with strips of LEDs to illuminate the forecourt without recourse to extraneous lamps. A deep and narrow passage leads to the entry with is bright yellow metal awning that hums like a tuning fork in the rain. In creating this alternation of openness and compression as an overture to the soaring volume of the living room, Brandon was inspired by a fortnight he had spent at the Alhambra in Granada, rising early to dodge the tour groups and sketch the masterly manipulation of space by fourteenth-century Islamic architects.

The architects put a lot of effort into hardening the house: the metal roof and black magnesium board siding protects the house from flying embers and it has a four-hour resistance to fire, way beyond what the county requires. The old foundations were replaced with 40 piers drilled into the hillside to resist seismic shocks. Trees shade the expansive windows and dead trunks were removed to improve the view. The house is self-sustaining and off the grid. All this gives it a good chance of surviving natural disasters in a remote location where help may be slow in coming.

The interior is lined with a light, warm-toned birch nautical plywood. Jorgensen was determined to mold the ceilings in three dimensions— much as Charles and Ray Eames labored to mold their classic plywood chairs—and he experimented with ways of achieving this by scoring and soaking the wood. The curvature is so subtle that it eludes the camera lens, but you feel it as one of the elements that makes the interior so calming. In the living room, which rises to 30 feet (9 m), the ceiling is out of the field of vision as you gaze through the room-height glazing. A breakfast nook tucked under the open-tread staircase offers an intimate counterpart to this lofty volume.

The primary suite occupies the northeast corner of the house on the upper level. "We wake up to a view of the valley and the sun is never in our face," says the wife. The view highlights certain trees, so the panorama is constantly changing, and when fog rolls into the valley you see objects emerging hazily as in a Chinese ink and brush drawing. There is no ambient light; on clear nights the sky is a starry dome.

1   Entry court
2   Entry
3   Dining area
4   Living area
5   Kitchen
6   Wine / pantry
7   Laundry / utility
8   Nook
9   Bedroom
10 Bathroom
11 Mechanical room
12 Terrace
13 Firepit
14 Landing
15 Primary bedroom
16 Primary dressing room
17 Primary bathroom
18 Study

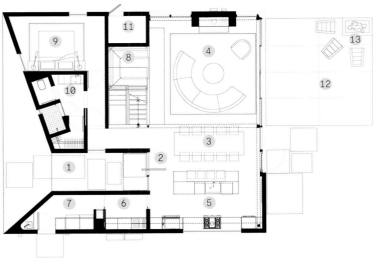

FIRST-FLOOR PLAN

SECOND-FLOOR PLAN

VIEWING TOWN & COUNTRY

CALIFORNIA HOUSES

VIEWING TOWN & COUNTRY

CALIFORNIA HOUSES

VIEWING TOWN & COUNTRY

Three Gables
Napa Valley

AIDLIN DARLING DESIGN

Wildfires have overtaken earthquakes as the chief hazard of living in California, especially in remote locations. Debra Grassgreen and Karl Knight faced that risk head-on when they commissioned Joshua Aidlin to design them a house amid the vineyards overlooking Napa Valley. Both had highly successful careers in San Francisco—she as a nationally renowned lawyer, he as an entrepreneur—but they wanted to indulge their shared passion for country living and cooking with produce they had grown themselves. For him it was a nod to his roots in the countryside of Wales, and their teenage son took to the experience. "We wanted a contemporary house that fit the landscape and would stand the test of time," said Grassgreen. A wildfire destroyed the house halfway through construction but, undeterred, they started over.

"After 30 years of practice we select clients with whom we can have a joyful collaboration," says Aidlin. "This 4,550-square-foot 422.7 m²] house was the product of a dialogue with two well-traveled people who had a clear vision of what they wanted without being prescriptive." The clients had bought the 10-acre property a decade before and vacationed there in a simple existing structure. Aidlin and his team followed their lead, camping out at the site and sketching concepts, as they do on every job. Inspiration came from the agrarian vernacular: a sophisticated reinterpretation of clustered barns. Here, the main house is pulled apart and a deck separates the living areas from the primary suite at the entry level. Two bedrooms are tucked in below. A garage is set at right angles to the house, and three attic spaces provide offices for each member of the family. Board-formed concrete walls and steeply pitched standing-seam metal roofs protect the house from flying embers, while sprinklers on the roof and around the perimeter shield the stained-black cedar siding from flames.

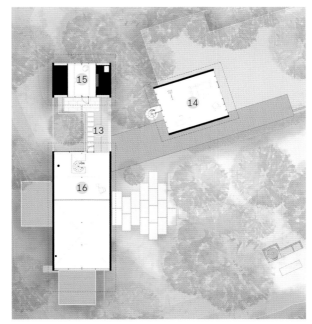

THIRD-FLOOR PLAN

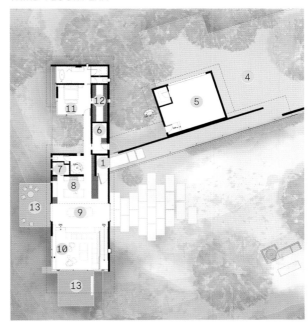

SECOND-FLOOR PLAN

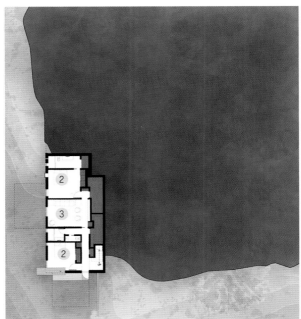

FIRST-FLOOR PLAN

1   Entry
2   Bedroom
3   Den
4   Car court
5   Garage
6   Mud room
7   Pantry
8   Kitchen
9   Dining area
10   Living area
11   Primary suite
12   Closet
13   Outdoor deck
14   Garage office
15   Office
16   Loft

The roofs project out to shade verandas at either end of the living area, and they give the house its name. The three gables are its most distinctive feature: an angular punctuation mark in the undulating landscape. Corten-steel walls enclose a sheltered walkway from the parking area to the house, creating an architectural promenade of compression and narrow glimpses beyond to build anticipation for the open airy house. Every window frames a distinct view and the owners' one regret is the loss of the oaks that clustered around the house when it was first designed but were incinerated in the fire. It would take generations to restore that bosky landscape, so instead they have planted olive and fruit trees alongside an infinity pool and a Corten-steel-clad workshop.

The hub of the house for the family and their many appreciative guests is the kitchen, a gleaming stainless-steel ensemble manufactured by Abimis for professional chefs. It is flanked by an open dining area and a dining terrace with the double-height sitting area beyond. Large glass windows to the east and west provide cross ventilation, and there are panoramic views of the countryside from every opening and deck. "In designing houses, we ask clients about activities, their thoughts on scale and how they like to use spaces," explains Aidlin. "They didn't want a living room in which they'd feel lost." The architects spent a lot of time calculating the height of that space and how it related to the open loft above the kitchen so that both felt intimate. Steel cross ties within the living room act as a scaling device, and the exposed roof vault suggests a canopy floating overhead. Oak floors, ceilings, and cabinets complement the exposed concrete and steel structure, as well as the pristine steel and bronze casework.

For Aidlin, a project like this draws on early memories of growing up in the country and how, during his first 10 years of practice in San Francisco he slept under the exposed joists of a Victorian attic. "We want to focus on multi-purpose spaces so we can shrink the size of the house," he says. "The computer allows us to work or catch up on correspondence in any room or outside."

CALIFORNIA HOUSES

Goto House
Napa County

IWAMOTOSCOTT ARCHITECTURE

Cellular Origami is the name Lisa Iwamoto and Craig Scott gave to the façade of a garage they designed for the University of California, San Francisco, and it could be used to describe the angular weekend house that tech engineer Ken Goto and his wife commissioned for a 10-acre site, an hour's drive from their residence in the city. Goto was familiar with the architects' work, having rented part of an office building they designed, and he asked for a glass house with four pods surrounding an inner courtyard. They would house a living area, primary suite, a bedroom for two young children to share and a multi-purpose space that would double as a guest bedroom. "We've always had a fascination with the alternation of solid and void," says Scott, "and, having lived on a remote mountain ranch, I share his love of rugged countryside."

The team presented three schemes to the client: an orthogonal block with a perforated-metal jacket, a break-out of the four pods, and a hollow hexagon, which evolved into the final design. The architects considered different locations before planting the house on a plateau with a sweeping view over Lake Berryessa, 100 feet (30.5 m) below. They had to demonstrate to the county planning office that the residence would not show up from a scenic route along the lake and would be well-protected from wildfires. The house is off the grid, relying on solar power and a spring, but the owner had to pay for a paved road to provide access for emergency services, delaying the start of construction.

The roof and side walls are clad in metal, while the entry and three inset decks are lined with engineered cedar over a fire-resistant substrate. The architects proposed to protect these with folding doors of metal mesh, which would also shade the glass from direct sun, but the owner found those unsightly, preferring to put film on the glass and block the sun with roll-down blinds. When a wildfire did rage through, a couple of years after completion, one corner of the house was scorched but the rest survived intact. To resist seismic shocks and compensate for loose soil, the house was mounted on an extra-thick reinforced-concrete slab. This tilts up at the edges, keeping snakes and scorpions at bay, and the house appears to hover over the ground.

The irregular hexagonal plan ensures that every room and deck has a different view and introduces a spatial complexity to this compact 2,230-square-foot (207.2 m²) retreat. The honed concrete floor with radiant heating ties the varied spaces together, and pocketing glass sliders open two sides of the living room. Angled recesses in the upward-sloping, paneled-oak ceilings conceal LED lighting. The diamond-plan inner court

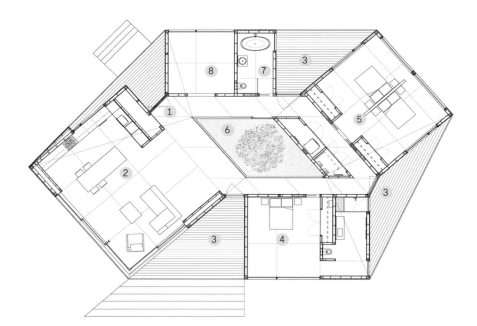

1 Entry
2 Living / dining / kitchen area
3 Covered deck
4 Primary bedroom suite
5 Child's bedroom
6 Courtyard
7 Guest bathroom
8 Guest bedroom

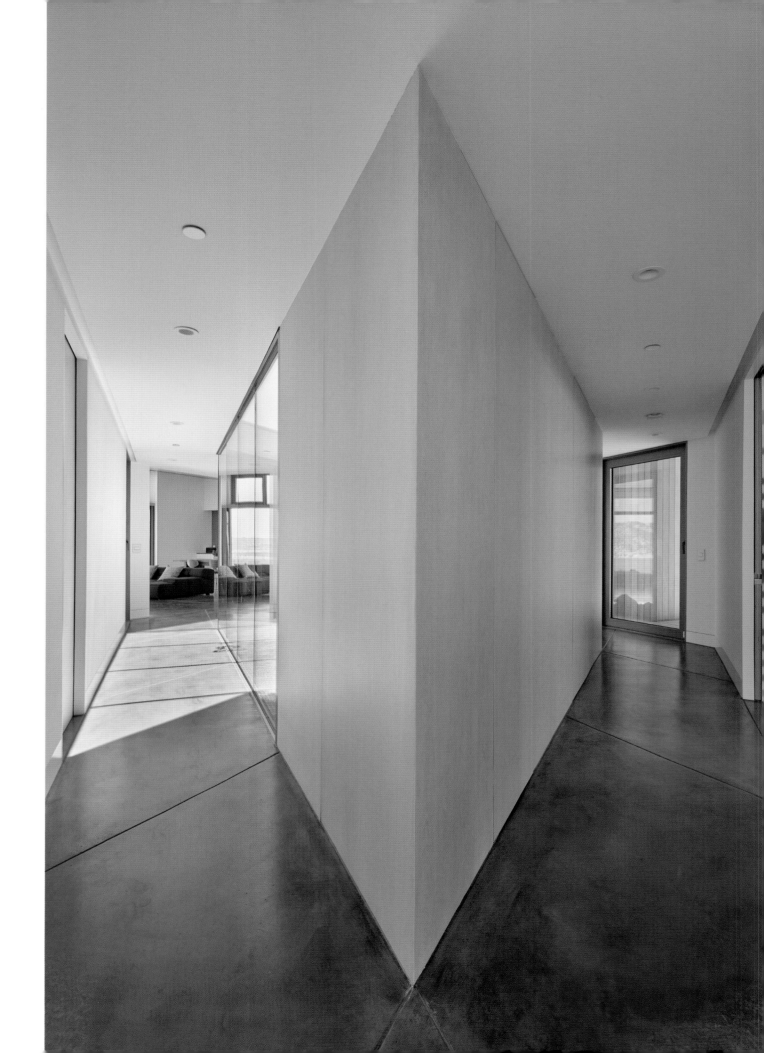

is lined with glass on three sides and is treated as a dry zen garden featuring a sapling surrounded by rocks and an expanse of gravel. As you walk around this central void, inner views appear and vanish, and the glass captures multiple reflections. A sharp wedge of whitened oak conceals mechanical services. As an electrical engineer, the owner devised a way of opening clerestory windows and cooling the interior while driving up from the city. A separate garage contains additional services and electrical storage batteries.

IwamotoScott applied a similar strategy of folding a façade to capture views with an infill house they designed on spec for a builder in the Noe Valley district of San Francisco. The angles relate to the different setbacks of neighboring houses, and the vertical cladding of clear cedar boards and black spacer boards has an affinity with the subtler modeling of the bay window on Hidden House (see p. 110). In a trefoil exhibition pavilion the architects designed for a planned development near the Chinese metropolis of Chengdu, the angles mutate into graceful curves, extending like the petals of a flower.

The folded façade of an infill house that IwamotoScott designed in the Noe Valley district of San Francisco.

VIEWING TOWN & COUNTRY

Hilltops
Silver Lake

BESTOR ARCHITECTURE

In a few fortunate communities, neighbors still converse over the garden fence; on this site there is a lively dialogue between a streamline classic, the Lipetz House designed by Raphael Soriano in 1936, and an angular new house designed by Barbara Bestor to step down the adjoining slope. Like John Friedman, whose JArzm House is nearby (see p. 204), she wanted to give the house a sense of openness without blocking anyone else's views. And the goal was to achieve a dramatic contrast between old and new. "Rather than a retro version of the Soriano I wanted natural forms that would play off his machine imagery but have enough ambiguity that they could be read in different ways," she explains. "Some might view the sequence of five pitched roofs as a village, others as an echo of the mountains beyond." The abstract sculptures of Joel Shapiro were another source of inspiration.

Erich Mendelsohn might have created the bowed glass bay of the old house in Weimar Berlin or later in Tel Aviv; in fact, it was Soriano's assured debut, and its principal feature was the music room for concert pianist Helen Lipetz. Bill Macomber and his wife Annie Weisman cherished this treasure but needed more space for their two young daughters, so they selected Bestor to give them a 3,000-square-foot (279 m²) house on the next-door lot, and they now rent the Soriano to an architectural aficionado.

A drive leads down from a narrow twisty road to a walled forecourt that doubles as an event space and a garage. Beyond lies a long living room that opens through glass sliders onto a pool terrace, and half a level down are three bedrooms. Nothing could be simpler than this U-plan and half-floor shift of level, and construction was tightly budgeted, but Bestor has made inspired use of limited resources. It may have helped that she and her team were designing this house while restoring John Lautner's Silvertop, a modern masterpiece that occupies a similar site, but on a much grander scale. They have distilled the essence of that complex structure in a few simple moves.

Materiality is one. Tactile poured-concrete walls anchor the house to the hillside, and the Douglas fir formwork was sandblasted to bring out the grain. Customized wood scissor trusses were prefabricated, and the parts were bolted together to frame the five bays of varied size. The exterior of the roof is wrapped in a membrane of white thermoplastic that deflects sunlight and protects from wildfires. Spaciousness is another defining characteristic. The lofty, angled ceilings make the principal room feel much larger than it is, as do the vistas from expansive glazing to either side. The indoor–outdoor flow of space and the feeling of seclusion make this a paradise for children and a soothing retreat for busy professionals (he has a post-production company; she is a writer-producer). As Weissman says, "We love to entertain and there's a continuum between cooking for friends in the kitchen and playing in the pool."

Solar panels on the south slopes of the roof cover a significant portion of energy needs. Overhangs and the separation of up to 3 feet (0.9 m) between the upper and lower roof planes provide good insulation while concealing ductwork. North-facing skylights are deep-set for shade and to vent hot air, but the stiff winds at this elevation offer natural ventilation when all the windows are open. The house is full of telling details, from the bold yellow entry door (a Bestor signature) to the subtle pink of the kitchen, which can be curtained off with a patterned fabric left over from the architect's Trina Turk design showroom. A snug media room opens out of the kitchen, and high above the cabinets is a hideaway for one of the girls. The pool changing room beside the entry does double duty as a powder room, with outside and inside doors, and the porthole window references the streamline neighbor. In a further nod to the context, the pool provides a visual link to the reservoir below.

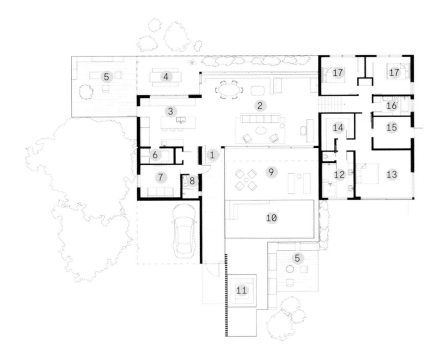

1   Entry
2   Living / dining area
3   Kitchen
4   Outdoor dining area
5   Firepit lounge
6   Pantry
7   Media room
8   Powder room
9   Pool patio deck
10 Pool
11 Spa
12 Primary bathroom
13 Primary bedroom
14 Primary closet
15 Office
16 Bathroom
17 Bedroom

CALIFORNIA HOUSES

VIEWING TOWN & COUNTRY

LR2 House
Pasadena

MONTALBA ARCHITECTS

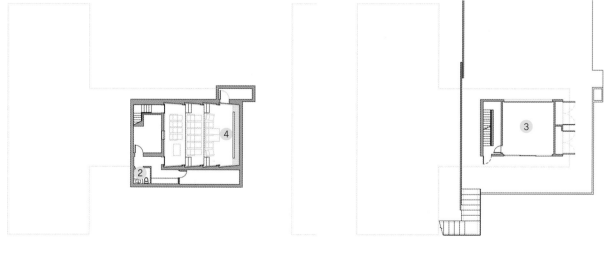

BASEMENT PLAN   FIRST-FLOOR PLAN

CALIFORNIA HOUSES

There are still pockets of wilderness in the vast sprawl of Los Angeles, and David Montalba has built a house that responds to a steep canyon, the native chaparral, and a sweeping view beyond. It hugs the slope next door to a smaller house he designed for the same client in the early years of his practice. At the outset of the commission, architect and client walked the site and found a little goat trail that commanded views and led down to the house that used to be there. Montalba tried to keep the spirit of that trail in the circulation route through the new house as he developed three concepts in massing models and did full renderings for two of them. Client and architect selected the one in which volumes cascade down the hillside and cantilever out.

That was the start of a four-year struggle with the Pasadena Planning Department, which imposes extraordinarily tight restrictions on hillside development. A less determined architect might have proposed a more conventional solution. But, as Montalba insists, "life is too short to do mundane work and exceptional clients inspire us." He draws on a deep immersion in the architectural culture of southern California and decades of experience in building there.

Terraces, balconies, and walkways add 2,300 square feet (213.7 m²) to the 4,200 square feet (390.2 m2) of enclosed space on four levels. Expansive windows and glass sliders are framed by chamfered rainscreens of black concrete board clipped to the studs. Rectilinear volumes are set at right angles to each other, breaking up the mass and creating a sense of levitation. The upper level cantilevers off the slope, the middle level extends forward and is supported by the garage. A screening room occupies the basement, and a flight of steps winds up the slope beside a natural creek to the second-floor entry. The apparent simplicity of the composition conceals the complexity of construction with its caissons, retaining walls, and steel structural frame. As Montalba notes with a touch of hyperbole, "the structure underpinning this house could support a three-way freeway overpass." One is reminded of John Lautner's prolonged fight to secure approval for the daringly engineered driveway of his Silvertop house in Silver Lake, back in the 1960s.

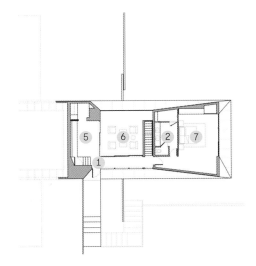

SECOND-FLOOR PLAN

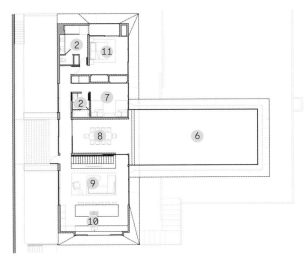

THIRD-FLOOR PLAN

1 Entry
2 Bathroom
3 Garage
4 Screening room
5 Office / gallery
6 Outdoor terrace
7 Bedroom
8 Outdoor dining terrace
9 Living room
10 Kitchen
11 Primary bedroom

The second and third floors feel self-contained, with a mixture of living and sleeping spaces that include guest suites, a gym, and a home office, as well as generous outdoor areas for entertaining. The sharply angled façades reflect Montalba's love of Swiss precision, dating from his early years in that country to the office he now maintains in Lausanne (his family moved to California while he was still a small boy, but he has kept his dual citizenship). Plantings mask neighboring buildings, which include the Rose Bowl stadium, and the top floor offers the sensation of floating high in the air, while rising only 30 feet (9 m) above the street. There is a feeling of separation from the landscape even though the house is firmly rooted in the ground.

Within, the blond plywood floors and millwork give the rooms a relaxed mid-twentieth-century feel, and that is reinforced by the owner's choice of classic modern furniture by Charles & Ray Eames and Eero Saarinen, Mies van der Rohe and Hans Wegner. At every point there is a different view, close-up or away to the San Gabriel Mountains. Thus, the house achieves a balance of distance and proximity, intimacy and flight, enriching the experience of moving through it. The interior is infused with natural light from every direction, but comes most alive at night when the rooms appear like giant lanterns suspended across the darkened slope.

VIEWING TOWN & COUNTRY

Will Gluck House
Sherman Oaks

GLUCK +

Peter Gluck heads an architectural firm with over 50 years of experience in design and construction, so he can quickly grasp the potential of a challenging site. His son William, a Hollywood writer–director, waited two years to purchase a steep plot of land leading off Mulholland Drive. The former owner had considered it unbuildable, but "the concept of the house came to me 15 minutes after I started to sketch," recalls the architect, a New Yorker who then had to navigate the labyrinth of regulations that impede creative talents in Los Angeles.

The basic idea remained unchanged: a rectilinear glass-walled pavilion canopied by a roof plane that projects out on all four sides to block summer sun, sitting atop private spaces excavated from the hillside. The living area above and the bedrooms below both command sweeping views over the San Fernando Valley and the range of hills that divide it from the flatlands of Los Angeles to the south. Trees block the only house in sight, so that it is easy to imagine one is living in a wilderness rather than a metropolis. Philip Johnson built a nearly windowless guest house a short stroll from his celebrated Glass House in New Canaan, Connecticut; Peter Gluck has achieved a similar complementary relationship of exposure and enclosure within a single volume.

In LA you are allowed to excavate only a limited amount of earth from hillsides, but the space below the ground-level pavilion does not count towards the total, so the lower level can extend far beyond its perimeter. That greatly reduces the impact of the 7,000-square-foot (650.3 m²) house, which the owner likens to a Trojan Horse, concealing its true identity. As you approach, the down ramp to the garage is the only hint that there is more to the house than first appears. The green roof over the lower floor is watertight and glass inserts pull in natural light. Since the bedrooms have windows on only one side, that allows the upper floor to be fully glazed and still meet the state's exacting energy requirements.

As the doors can be opened for cross ventilation, the house rarely requires mechanical air conditioning, even at the height of summer when daytime temperatures can exceed 100 degrees Fahrenheit (38 degrees Celsius).

The roof plane is tapered at the edges and supported on slender steel columns: upright to carry the load and splayed to absorb seismic shifts. The design review board rejected the idea of a flat roof, not for stylistic reasons, but out of concern that it would be used as a dance floor. By folding up two corners, the architects were able to enlarge the field of view and make the roof seem even more airborne. The apparent lightness is deceptive, for it is a complicated structure of steel beams and a wood frame, 20-inches (50.8 cm) thick and heavily insulated. A single interior column supplements the perimeter supports, and the lower level rests on 50 piles.

The Gluck house has an elemental quality, achieving a harmonious balance of earth and air. Hawks wheel overhead and the freeway traffic far below is muted. The hills shimmer in the heat of summer and dissolve in the morning mists. The upper level is suffused with light and leads out on all sides—to a grassy glass-railed terrace, a pool and a drought-resistant garden of succulents. Wood battens enclose the hearth, powder room, storage cabinets, and a tiny study that William can close off in order to write undisturbed. These containers—oak on the outside, maple within—project through the glass like paniers, heightening the sense of transparency to either side. The kitchen and dining area open onto an expansive living area with custom-designed modular furniture that can be reconfigured for entertaining. In contrast, the downstairs spaces—four bedrooms opening off a spinal corridor, an office, and a sybaritic screening room—are snug and dimly lit, with maple floors and cabinetry. There, the inspiration comes not from nature but from Jun'ichirō Tanizaki's classic essay, *In Praise of Shadows* (1933).

1	Entry
2	Bedroom
3	Office
4	Primary bedroom
5	Outdoor terrace
6	Walk-in closet
7	Theater
8	Mud room
9	Garage
10	Gym
11	Dining area
12	Living area
13	Lounge
14	Kitchen
15	Pantry
16	Pool
17	Cactus garden

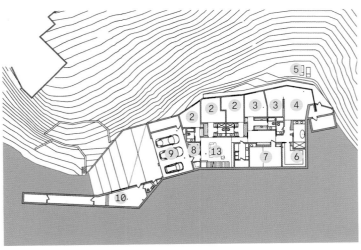

LOWER-FLOOR PLAN

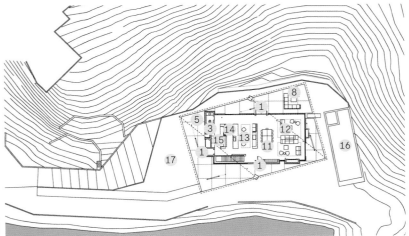

UPPER-FLOOR PLAN

CALIFORNIA HOUSES

The Architects

ROBIN DONALDSON worked with Morphosis Architects before founding SHUBINDONALDSON ARCHITECTS with RUSSELL SHUBIN in 1991 and opening his studio in Montecito. His creative drive advances the firm's design ethos and leads its research and development efforts, furthering its investigations into architectural drawing and representation, material fabrication, and the integration of building and landscape. Donaldson serves on community and planning advisory boards across southern California.
pp. 16–27
shubindonaldson.com

ANNE FOUGERON launched FOUGERON ARCHITECTURE in San Francisco in 1985. The firm has a strong commitment to clarity of thought, design integrity, and the quality of architectural detail. She is dedicated to finding the perfect balance between architectural idea and built form, emphasizing the importance of natural light, integral ornament, and the visual and tactile nature of materials.
pp. 28–35
fougeron.com

GEHRY PARTNERS, LLP, is a full-service architectural firm with extensive international experience in the design and construction of academic, museum, theater, performance, and commercial projects. Founded in 1962 by Frank Gehry, the firm's mission is to raise architecture to the level of art, while creating buildings that meet the client's functional and budgetary needs.
pp. 36–43
foga.com

JIM JENNINGS – The projects of San Francisco-based JIM JENNINGS ARCHITECTURE—institutional and commercial, with residential forming the nucleus—have garnered numerous honors, including the Maybeck Award, AIA California's highest individual honor. In 2008 the American Academy of Arts and Letters honored Jennings's four decades of practice with

its Academy Award for Architecture, citing his "unwavering modernist sensibility and a portfolio defined by a coolly sensuous rigor."
pp. 44–51
jimjenningsarchitecture.com

MARK DZIEWULSKI launched his international practice in Manhattan in 1990 and has since been based in San Francisco, London, and, currently, in France. In addition to houses, the practice creates significant projects in the public realm, based on the rigorous expression of strong design principles. Its work has been praised for its sensitivity to context and for creating community landmarks.
pp. 52–57
dzarchitect.com

JOHNSTON MARKLEE – Since its founding in 1998 in Los Angeles by Sharon Johnston and Mark Lee, this practice has assembled an internationally recognized portfolio distinguished by a conceptual approach to design. The structures and atmospheres that have come to define the practice's work are subtle, yet deliberate contributions to its immediate environs as well as the larger cultural realm.
pp. 58–65
johnstonmarklee.com

MICHAEL MALTZAN ARCHITECTURE is a Los Angeles architecture and urban design practice founded by Michael Maltzan in 1995. The studio is focused on cross-disciplinary partnerships to integrate social and environmental sustainability, construction innovation, and architectural form. The practice has been recognized with five Progressive Architecture awards, 47 citations from the AIA, and the Rudy Bruner Foundation's Gold Medal for Urban Excellence.
pp. 66–73
mmaltzan.com

CRAIG STEELY is a California- and Hawaii-based architect, and his buildings have been described as hybrids of those two

places. They embrace the realities of the environment and our separation/connection to it, while focusing on a singular architecture rooted in context. Besides Hawaii, his houses are located in Mexico and along the California coast, from Sea Ranch to San Francisco and Big Sur.
pp. 74–79
craigsteely.com

PETER TOLKIN + SARAH LORENZEN ARCHITECTURE (TOLO) works on a variety of project types, including houses, workspaces, retail, and arts-oriented projects, such as galleries and large-scale art installations. Since its founding in 2000, the Los Angeles-based studio has been recognized in awards and publications for the social content of its work and for its spatial and material inventiveness.
pp. 80–87
toloarchitecture.com

KOJI TSUTSUI – The practice of KOJI TSUTSUI ARCHITECT & ASSOCIATES was established in Tokyo in 2004 and San Francisco in 2010. Tsutsui has designed numerous projects around the world while observing economic and architectural developments in multiple countries. He incorporates local cultures and building technologies into his designs to create a new generation of lasting, sustainable architecture.
pp. 88–93
kt-aa.com

DOUGLAS BURNHAM established ENVELOPE A+D in Berkeley in 2002 as an idea-driven architecture and activation studio. The firm is recognized for its pioneering work in transforming underutilized places, for crafting environments attuned to the dynamics of contemporary culture, and for realizing an equitable and compelling built environment. It engages with a diversity of issues relating to architecture, communities, public programs, and curation.
pp. 94–99
envelopead.com

OONAGH RYAN founded ORA in the Arts District of Los Angeles in 2014 as a creative architecture and design studio. Its diverse portfolio is a mix of playful and practical, exploring the intersection of space, light, quality, craft, economy, and longevity. The team collaborates with organizations and individuals with ambitious goals and ideas. Its work speaks to the people it is built for, the times we live in and how we live.
ora.la

OGRYDZIAK PRILLINGER ARCHITECTS (OPA) was founded in 2004 by Luke Ogrydziak and Zoë Prillinger in San Francisco. They see architecture as a powerful innovative force for creating a better future. Built work, driven by ideas, expands what is possible to think and how to live. For OPA, architecture is always about freedom. Every project, private or public, is personal—a joint exploration with clients and communities to challenge constraints and transform potential.
oparch.net

RAVEEVARN CHOKSOMBATCHAI founded VEEV DESIGN, her San Francisco practice, in 2005 as an interdisciplinary design studio. She and her associates work with a consistent focus on spatial and material investigation, engaging with conventional methods of construction and finding new ways of using off-the-shelf materials. She seeks to create an architecture that reflects users' needs and desires, the physical landscape, and the wisdom of local construction methods.
veevdesign.com

STANLEY SAITOWITZ has practiced and taught architecture for more than 45 years. Born in South Africa, he received his Masters in Architecture at UC Berkeley in 1977 and established NATOMA ARCHITECTS in San Francisco. He has completed numerous residential, commercial, and institutional buildings and projects in California and across the US, and has received many awards.
saitowitz.com

GRIFFIN ENRIGHT ARCHITECTS is an award-winning, interdisciplinary Los Angeles-based firm creating institutional, cultural, and residential projects, nationally and abroad. The firm was founded by Margaret Griffin, FAIA, and John Enright, FAIA, as a collaborative design practice that explores new prospects for the built environment through the integration of architectural, urban, landscape, and interior design.
griffinenrightarchitects.com

DAVID HERTZ, FAIA, is the founder and president of Studio of Environmental Architecture (SEA). Like Syndesis—his first practice, founded in 1983—SEA has particular expertise in regenerative design. In 2018 Hertz led his team to win the Water Abundance XPRIZE and was recently awarded the 2022 Cooper Hewitt, Smithsonian Design Museum's National Design Award for Climate Action.
davidhertzfaia.com

ERIC OWEN MOSS ARCHITECTS (EOMA) was founded in 1973. The Culver City-based office has completed projects in the US and around the world. There are 22 published monographs on the work of the firm, and EOMA projects have garnered over 150 local, national, and international design awards. Moss has held teaching positions at major universities around the world including the Southern California Institute of Architecture (SCI-Arc), where he also served as director from 2002 to 2015.
ericowenmoss.com

KONING EIZENBERG ARCHITECTURE is known for its focus on inclusive, sustainable neighborhoods and for an award-winning portfolio of innovative housing, community, and educational buildings. Established in 1981 in Santa Monica by Hank Koning and Julie Eizenberg, the practice has grown to include a design and technical team who are similarly invested in humanist values, an environmental agenda, and a collaborative approach to design.
kearch.com

EYRC ARCHITECTS – Working within the tradition of California modernism, Ehrlich Yanai Rhee Chaney creates buildings that draw on the sustainable wisdom of vernacular architecture from Africa and Japan. The practice's work applies the latest technologies to maximize indoor–outdoor living. People connect to nature and each other in contemplative spaces that nourish the soul.
eyrc.com

FREELANDBUCK is a Los Angeles- and New York City-based office founded and led by Brennan Buck and David Freeland. Established in 2010, the practice makes buildings, spaces, and objects that engage the public through layers of meaning, illusion, and visual effect. The firm's architecture and public artwork is notable for its visual richness and intricate spatial sequences, and it has won several major awards.
freelandbuck.com

KEVIN DALY ARCHITECTS was established in Los Angeles in 1990 and now has a second office in New York. It is focused on craft, construction systems, and material research, and its work interweaves innovation in technology and fabrication, new approaches to sustainability and urbanism, and a commitment to livability and economy. The firm's award-winning portfolio includes educational, residential, and institutional projects, ranging from single rooms to master plans.
kevindalyarchitects.com

KATY BARKAN is a Los Angeles-based designer who founded her practice, NOW HERE, in 2017, and is on the faculty of UCLA's department of architecture and urban design. She received the Rome Prize in Architecture in 2020, and has exhibited and published her work widely, including at the Venice Biennale.
nownowherehere.com

TOM KUNDIG is a principal of OLSON KUNDIG, a Seattle-based design practice now in its sixth decade. Kundig has won some of the world's highest honors and is known for his contextual approach to design. His buildings are a direct response to place and include houses, hospitality projects, workplaces, and adaptive re-use around the world.
olsonkundig.com

JOHN FRIEDMAN ALICE KIMM ARCHITECTS (JFAK) is a Los Angeles-based practice dedicated to producing architecture

THE ARCHITECTS

as a public good. With projects spanning educational, institutional, residential, and civic typologies, and with a particular emphasis on the crisis of homelessness in their home city, JFAK's work has been recognized for its formal inventiveness, playfulness, and a drive toward working with and through the built environment.
pp. 204–15
jfak.net

XTEN ARCHITECTURE is an award-winning international architecture firm based in Los Angeles and Sissach, Switzerland, specializing in custom residential, cultural, and commercial buildings. Founded in 2000, it is now led by Monika Haefelfinger and Scott Utterstrom. Its distinctive designs are characterized by sculptural forms, refined materials, advanced structural strategies, and sustainable technologies.
pp. 216–23
xtenarchitecture.com

MICHAEL KOVAC DESIGN STUDIO is a Los Angeles-based architecture and design practice focused on creating meticulously crafted, highly personalized projects. Founded in 1988, the studio soon earned commissions for high-end health clubs, commercial spaces, and detail-rich residences. Years later, the studio's goal is still simple: to imbue each project with meaning and enduring quality.
pp. 224–33
kovacdesignstudio.com

FREDERICK FISHER AND PARTNERS designs exceptional spaces for the practice and exhibition of art, as well as for interdisciplinary study. Fisher is driven by his liberal arts background to treat architecture as an inclusive exploration. He has won a succession of honors for his work, including the 2013 Gold Medal of the LA chapter of the American Institute of Architects, and he is a Fellow of the American Academy in Rome in addition to his academic appointments in the US.
pp. 234–41
fisherpartners.net

SANDER ARCHITECTS is a Los Angeles-based practice established by Whitney Sander to advance the cause of green residential architecture. Early on, the firm developed the concept of Hybrid Construction, combining a factory-built structural frame with custom infill.

Few architects have employed prefab technology in such inventive ways.
pp. 242–49
sander-architects.com

KIERANTIMBERLAKE was founded in 1984 as an internationally renowned, full-service design and planning firm. Projects include the programming, planning, and design of new structures, as well as the conservation, renovation, and transformation of existing buildings, with special expertise in education, government, arts and culture, civic, and residential projects.
pp. 250–57
kierantimberlake.com

BRANDON JORGENSEN launched his design practice, ATELIER JORGENSEN, in 2011 in Napa. He previously studied with Tadao Ando and worked with SOM. Now he divides his time between California and Hawaii, designing houses that are tailored to clients and the sites. The team makes good use of technology, but is hands-on in its approach.
pp. 258–65
brandonjorgensen.com

AIDLIN DARLING DESIGN began in 1998 as the joint effort of Joshua Aidlin and David Darling. It has grown into an award-winning, San Francisco-based practice that explores design across a wide range of scales, programs, and disciplines. Its collaborative studio is a creative hub for an extended network of collaborators, working on residential commissions and a wide range of typologies.
pp. 266–73
aidlindarlingdesign.com

IWAMOTOSCOTT ARCHITECTURE was established in the San Francisco Bay Area by Lisa Iwamoto and Craig Scott in 2002. The practice is guided by the belief that each project, regardless of scope or scale, can achieve a unique design synthesis. The firm's work has gained widespread recognition and numerous awards for innovation in design. Both partners maintain academic careers alongside professional practice.
pp. 274–79
iwamotoscott.com

BESTOR ARCHITECTURE – Founded by Barbara Bestor in 1995, this Los Angeles-based practice has designed a number of award-winning projects including

headquarters for Beats by Dre and Snap, Inc., and other technology pioneers, Blackbirds, a groundbreaking typology for dense housing in Echo Park, and a variety of experimental residences and commercial establishments. The varied, creative, and aesthetically progressive body of work expands the territory of architecture into atmospheric urbanism.
pp. 280–85
bestorarchitecture.com

MONTALBA ARCHITECTS was founded by David Montalba in 2004 as an international practice with offices in Los Angeles and Lausanne, creating architecture and urban design in the US and around the world. The firm's projects emphasize experiences by creating environments that are socially responsive and aesthetically progressive, notably in a succession of houses.
pp. 286–93
montalbaarchitects.com

GLUCK+ – Founded by Peter Gluck in New York in 1972, this is an internationally renowned architecture and construction firm that has won many awards. Its work ranges from single houses to residential and commercial mixed-use developments, as well as institutional and educational projects. The practice is recognized for expanding the role of the architect and has been widely published.
pp. 294–99
gluckplus.com

Picture Credits

Brandon Arant 138, 140–44
Iwan Baan 16–21, 23–27, 36, 38–43, 66–69,
    71–73, 88–93
Richard Barnes 94–96, 98–99
Jeremy Bittman 224–33, back cover
Darren Bradley 74–79
Benny Chan 130–32, 134, 135 (bottom),
    136–37, 204–05, 207–15
Bruce Damonte 118–25, 127–28, 274–75,
    277–82, 284–85
Laura Doss 145
Joe Fletcher 6, 22, 28–35, 44–47, 49–51,
    110–11, 113–17, 258–59, 261–65
Sam Frost 219
Art Gray 135 (top)
Tim Griffith 250–52, 253 (top), 264–67
David Hartwell 80–87
Hufton & Crow 112
Tim Hursley 296
Kyle Jeffers 253 (bottom)
Steve King 216–17, 220–23
Nic Lehoux 194 (bottom), 196–201, 203
Aaron Leitz 4–5, 192–93, 194 (top), 202
Nico Marques front cover, 52–53, 55–57,
    182–83
Matthew Millman 3, 160–67, 266–73
Courtesy Eric Owen Moss 146–47, 149–51
Steve Proehl 129
Sharon Risedorph 242–49
Kevin Scott 287–93
Eric Staudenmaier 58–61, 63–65, 100–07,
    152–59, 168–75
Tim Street-Porter 234–35, 237–41
Paul Vu 294–95, 298–99
Joshua White 176–81, 184–89

Michael Webb is a Los Angeles-based writer who has authored 30 books on architecture and design, while editing and contributing texts to many more. Three titles were published by Thames & Hudson: *Architects' Houses* (2018), *Building Community: New Apartment Architecture* (2017), and *The City Square* (1990). Michael has also written for leading journals in the US, Europe, and Asia. Growing up in London, he worked at *The Times* and *Country Life* before moving to the US. He was awarded an honorary membership in the Los Angeles chapter of the American Institute of Architects and was named Chevalier de l'Ordre des Arts et des Lettres for services to French culture.

Many thanks to Thames & Hudson, especially to Augusta Pownall for launching this survey, to Catherine Hooper for her sensitive copy editing, and to both for steering the project to completion. I also thank Lucas Dietrich for his constant support and encouragement, and Praline for their exemplary design. To the architects, photographers, and homeowners who offered their generous cooperation, I express my deepest appreciation. M.W.

On the cover
FRONT Wave House, Malibu, Mark Dziewulski Architect (see p. 52). Photo: Nico Marques
BACK Casa per Amici, Santa Monica, Michael Kovac Design Studio (see p. 225). Photo: Jeremy Bittman

This book follows the US convention of using "first floor" to describe what in British English is termed "ground floor."

First published in the United Kingdom in 2024 by
Thames & Hudson Ltd, 181A High Holborn, London WC1V 7QX

First published in the United States of America in 2024 by
Thames & Hudson Inc., 500 Fifth Avenue, New York, New York 10110

California Houses: Creativity in Context © 2024 Thames & Hudson Ltd, London

Text © 2024 Michael Webb

Designed by Praline (David Tanguy, Maëlle Christien)

British Library Cataloguing-in-Publication Data
A catalogue record for this book is available from the British Library

Library of Congress Control Number 2023949305

ISBN 978-0-500-02712-7

Printed and bound in China by Toppan Leefung Printing Limited

Be the first to know about our new releases, exclusive content, and author events by visiting
thamesandhudson.com
thamesandhudsonusa.com
thamesandhudson.com.au